34-2637

5-3-63

PRE-FEUDAL ENGLAND
The Jutes

PRE-FEUDAL ENGLAND

THE JUTES

By

J. E. A. JOLLIFFE

BARNES & NOBLE, Inc., New York

Publishers · Booksellers · Since 1873

First Published by Oxford University Press in 1933

FIRST EDITION 1933
REPRINTED 1962

Published by Frank Cass & Company Ltd.,
10 Woburn Walk, London, W.C.1

This book has been printed in Great Britain by
offset litho at Taylor Garnett Evans & Co. Ltd,
Watford, Herts, and bound by them

To
A. *and* E. J.,

PREFACE

THE original purpose of which the following pages are the result was that of finding some intelligible scheme of life and government in the pre-feudal phase of English history. It has always been evident that the thirteenth century surveys were written by men who saw the country through the eyes of feudalism, and equally evident that feudalism presupposes all kinds of facts, theories and relations which cannot be transplanted into the sixth, seventh and eighth centuries.

But, with a great deal that is evidently medieval, almost every survey preserves at least a few terms and practices which have a ring of antiquity about them. The old, with the instinctive conservatism of country life, persists in custom long after its meaning has been forgotten.

It was with the intention of gathering together such survivals in some one quarter of England that this inquiry was begun. The choice of Kent was a purely arbitrary one, dictated by the peculiar richness of the records preserved at Canterbury and by the unrivalled series of the Kentish codes and charters, and if there is anything of value in the result, it is in the carrying of our knowledge of English life into a fresh phase of civilization, in rediscovering the habit of government and social life, albeit in only the smallest of the kingdoms, in that darkest age of all between the settlement and the end of the eighth century.

If the institutions of primitive Kent are indeed such as I have seen them, it seems to me that we have a useful model to guide us in restoring the earliest past of England as a whole. The type is a simple one, answering needs and habits of life that must have been widely spread, and it should be elastic enough to conform to most, if not all, of the varieties of custom found in England. For that reason it is upon the form of this primitive society rather than upon its extension that I should wish consideration to weigh. The question of a south-eastern unity of custom imposed itself upon my original purpose, and was secondary to it.

A very short inquiry showed that Kent, although we know it as a separate kingdom, could not be treated in isolation. Characteristics which at first seemed most definitely Kentish soon proved to be shared by Sussex, Surrey, and Hampshire and, unless a false picture of the south-eastern area were to be given, it became necessary to determine how far this particular field of custom extended. In doing so I have been compelled to face the problem of a likeness in institutions which overrides the political system of the heptarchy, and which is certainly too primitive to have been acquired by borrowing in historical times. The solution which roused the fewest of many difficulties seemed to be that of the settlement of the whole south-eastern area by a people who shared a common custom from the beginning.

Whether this is the best or the only solution I must leave to others to decide. It is a consideration secondary to the primary intention of this study, the piercing, at one point at least, of the obstinate barrier of feudalism which has hitherto made it impossible to derive the beginnings of our constitution from the common political heritage of Teutonic Europe. It is this which is of importance, and, it seems to me, essentially new. I say that it is new, but it must be evident that work of this nature can only claim a partial originality. It is from the creative work of Round, Maitland, and Vinogradoff that the very method of modern research is borrowed, and some world such as I have outlined in Kent underlies much of Maitland's speculation about the earliest England, though he did not live to bring his thought to the test of practice. To all three I owe the debt that is incurred by all who come to study feudalism and its origins through their writings. More immediately my thanks are due to those who have helped me by advice and criticism. To Professor F. M. Powicke I am indebted for his unfailing encouragement and patience as editor, and for much invaluable guidance as to the general form of this study and upon many points of detail. My thanks are also due to the Officials of the Public Record Office, of the British Museum, and of the Libraries of the Deans and Chapters of Canterbury and Rochester, without whose help and direction my research would have been far more laborious and far less successful.

1933   J. E. A. J.

CONTENTS

MAPS

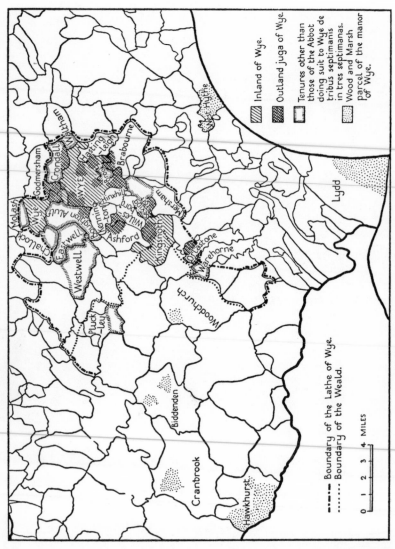

PLAN OF THE MANOR OF WYE
with approximate locations of the various tenures

Legend:
- Inland of Wye.
- Outland juga of Wye.
- Tenures other than those of the Abbot doing suit to Wye de tribus septimanis in tres septimanas.
- Wood and Marsh parcel of the manor of Wye.

-·-·- Boundary of the Lathe of Wye.
········· Boundary of the Weald.

0 1 2 3 4 MILES

I

KENT

(a) THE MANOR

THE map of southern England bears the traces of at least three racial settlements. In Oxfordshire, part of Berkshire, the north of Hampshire, and Wiltshire the villages are large and centralized. This is the true West Saxon land. But as we move outward from the central Saxon mass we find the village system less and less clearly defined, till on three sides, west, south, and east, it breaks up altogether and the hamlet becomes the predominant form of agricultural grouping. The hamlet areas of south-western Britain are clearly Celtic. They conform strictly with the general rules of Celtic agriculture, and in Devon and Cornwall they blend insensibly into that district of West Wales which remained Celtic in language and custom until recent times. The village areas of the middle Thames and the adjacent Midlands, on the other hand, are as clearly Saxon. Their crowded village sites and their common fields mark them as the homes of a typically Germanic people, and one in whose history social tradition has been unbroken.

If we accept this western racial boundary upon the witness of the map we shall find ourselves committed to a second. Not north and south, but irregularly east and west across the breadth of southern Wessex, runs another belt of hamlet settlements, thickest about the narrows of the Channel, but pushing inland towards the Thames and westwards to Hampshire till it thins away into spurs and salients which divide and sometimes encircle the sites of the villages. In the south-east, as in the west, Wessex was extending its power over a tenacious alien civilization, and though in this case the enemy was Teutonic, it was equally a nation of hamlet dwellers. Everywhere along the southern coast we may detect traces of this earlier people, and everywhere the relics of its custom display a common likeness. In Hampshire, Sussex, and Surrey it is often obscured by an overlayer of Saxon custom, and here and there interrupted by clearly defined enclaves of Saxon immigrants, but in Kent it has resisted all foreign elements.

Thus we have repeated in England that division which Maitzen brought to light between the eastern and western Germans of the mainland, and, though we may be cautious in ascribing it to a simple antagonism of race, it is the boundary between two of those bodies of custom which closely simulate the effects of race in their power of unification, of determining social and political life, and their millennial persistence.

Many local customs went to make up England. There is a Danish law, a Mercian law, a Saxon law, and all three are recognizable variations a hundred years after the Norman Conquest. There is a northern custom, half Welsh, half Anglian. There are provincial areas upon the Welsh border and in Cornwall, where Welsh and English custom mingle and still give rise to peculiar conditions of tenure. No instance of such divergence is so striking as that of Kent. Here we have the one local custom which had the strength to maintain itself against that Angevin crown which extinguished so many legal provinces to make an English common law. Gavelkind, the partible inheritance of land, which was the custom of the peasantry of Kent before the Norman Conquest, became the common law of Kent after it, and as such was pleadable in the king's courts. So much is recognized in every law-book and is a commonplace of every economic history. Yet it is doubtful whether the full implications of the fact have been realized. Little effort has been made to see Kent as a distinct national entity with possible analogies in the custom of the neighbouring provinces. To do so is the purpose of these pages.

Our first impression of early society in the south-east is one of disintegration, even of chaos. The lines of civil and ecclesiastical administration, of agricultural life, cross and contradict each other. The manor, so homogeneous elsewhere, is here a jumble of lands and jurisdictions without order, principle, or unity. The history of Kent has been very different from that slow unfolding of nationhood which has led the West Saxon people to a feudalism expressing and fortifying their proper qualities. Within 300 years Kent has suffered three conquests which have destroyed her political system and shaken her social life. The foundations and something of the superstructure have held good, but they are patched with Saxon and again with Norman custom. It is not surprising, therefore, that we find the feudalism of Kent to be rigid, artificial, full of contradictions and of unresolved elements of an older and freer custom, that its feudal aristocracy failed to gain a complete hold upon the peasantry or to adjust itself to the framework of public administration. The Kent of the Middle Ages is a foreign makeshift, its manorial superstructure thrown up hastily and setting clumsily to the native foundations.

Purely Teutonic as Kentish civilization seems to be, the manors of Kent are more like those of Wales than of Oxford and Berkshire, but the principle of their difference is hard to put into a phrase. Perhaps we may borrow the terms of the constitutional historian, and say that the Midland manor is unitary and that of the south-east federative. The term 'unitary' does, indeed, express two of the deepest characteristics of the Saxon manor—its unity and concentration. It is these that have scored the regular chequer of the fields in furrows which depict the persistent communism of village life as in a map. Community is writ upon the fields. The huddled, central mass of the homesteads is the dwelling-place of a group of neighbours. Around it stretch the fields, unbroken by hedge or fence, for each man's lot has been divided and scattered, so that each may have his share of good land and bad. The ploughs of the township plough them in common, one man's acres with another's. If we could look down upon it from above we should see the Saxon village as a diagram of ideal unity and co-operation, expressed in the varying reality of the countryside. Lordship and community form a single, compact whole.

The lowest unit of Domesday Kent is the manor, as it is in the other English provinces, and the existence of something worthy of the name of manor must be our preliminary hypothesis if we are to approach the subject through the minds of those best placed in time to judge. Assuming, then, that they are the natural units of the Kentish system, let us see what appearance is made upon the map by the manors of Domesday.

The Abbot of Battle's manor of Wye is typical in form, and its fortunes can be followed over some twelve centuries of history. At once we are faced by a fact alien from the orderly system of the Midlands. Wye changes its nature and its function in the land from century to century as feudalism advances. It is greatest in its beginnings, a royal town. We first meet with it in a charter of Ethelbert II of Kent,[1] *villa regalis quae nominatur Wyth*, an important place in the independent kingdom. It is a *cyninges tun*, in the especial peace of the king,[2] a centre of administration and the seat of a king's reeve. Other early charters strengthen our impression that its authority extended over a wide range of territory and over a considerable population.[3] In Domesday we find it giving its name to one of the six lathes, Wiuuart Lest, the lathe of the Wywara or men of Wye, an area of some 100 square miles assessed at 80 *sulungs*, with the right of summoning the courts of many hundreds and of enjoying the king's profits from their pleas. With the Norman Conquest its decline begins. On the foundation of Battle the Conqueror granted it to the Abbot shorn of much of its ancient jurisdiction. The lathe over which it once presided was reconstituted, and dropped the name of Wye for that of Sherwinhope, while the ancient name, with the *villa regalis*, passed to the endowment of the memorial Abbey, as the *manerium de Wi* with diminished powers.[4] It will hardly be questioned that this use of *manerium* is a Norman generalization and an unhappy one. Wye is a unit which has defied definition, though it has been called *villa regalis*, 'lathe', and 'manor' in turn. The complexity of Kentish tenure is such that no one term will really suffice to describe the heterogeneous bundle of lands, jurisdiction, and franchises which is all that survives of the ancient lathe of the Wywara.

As we see it on the map, Wye seems to be irreconcilable

[1] Birch, *Cartularium Saxonicum* (hereafter quoted as *Cart. Sax.*), 191.

[2] *Leges Ethelberti*, cap. 5.

[3] *Cart. Sax.* 449. The shire court still sometimes met at Wye in the reign of the Confessor; Kemble, Codex Diplomaticus Ævi Saxonici (hereafter quoted as *Cod. Dip.*) DCGLXXXIX: 'on wii ætforan ealra scyre'.

[4] Much of the Abbot's soke was restored at the end of the reign.

with any one principle of development such as is implied in the word 'manor'. It is more than a manor, more even than a hundred. Part of its lands, the fourteen *borghi* or boroughs[1] adjacent to Wye itself, do constitute a separate hundred and a large one,[2] but this is by no means all the ancient territory of the *villa regis*. The court of ancient demesne covers a much wider area, and has suit from the whole or part of some thirty parishes. The farthest limit of its resort is 19 miles to the westward at Cranbrook, while its most remote member to the south is 16 miles away at Lydd. The suit is from islands of jurisdiction intermixed with the land of other manors and other lords, and some lie many miles from the central court, but the Abbot could have crossed Kent from Wye, westward to the Weald or due south to the sea, without ever losing sight of his own land of this one manor, and there is hardly a parish of south-central Kent which does not contain some limb of Wye.

Even a superficial observer, with no other guide but the map and a list of the Abbey lands, sees that this is a problem which cannot be solved by the Midland formula of the manor-village. Here is a complex of land and lordship which considerably exceeds the hundred to which it gives its name, and one who knew something of the past might be inclined to think that the medieval liberty was a survival of the pre-Conquest lathe. The arable lands alone make up a considerable fraction of the lathe of Sherwinhope, and there are tracts of the manor lands which lie still farther from its centre. The core, to a radius of perhaps 6 miles about the curia, is agricultural, an alternation of arable land and pasture, interspersed in the proportion of the normal estate. It is part of the 80 measured sulungs of the lathe, and hidated at the usual value of settled land in the province. But beyond this, much of the land of Wye lies, and always has lain, outside the strict limits of lathe, the settled lands of Domesday, and has grown up out of the undeveloped waste of the kingdom. Besides the nucleus of agricultural land there are two other land-masses whose dependence upon the court of Wye can

1 The *borghus*, with certain differences, is the equivalent of the *decenna* of Wessex.
2 All or part of the modern parishes of Wye, Eastwell, Boughton Alulf, Crundall, Waltham, and Brook.

be carried back to remote antiquity, one at the extreme
western edge of the Abbot's lordship in the Weald[1] and the
other on the southern coast in the low lands of Romney.
Both these are unhidated in Domesday, and are set apart
from the primitive settlement-land of the Kentings. The
first is in Andred, that great woodland lying uncharted from
the eastern Rother to the Hampshire border, defying the
plough and excluding something like a third of Kent from
the common assessment. The second is meadow land by the
sea coast, where salt pastures provide the best of grazing for
the sheep. Both forest and marsh are public land of the folk,
a share of pasture in that national reserve of marsh and woodland which is an essential feature of the south-eastern settlement, and common in one form or another to all the older
estates of Kent, to many in Sussex, and to some in Hampshire and Surrey. The *communis silva*, in the great tract of
Andred and the lesser woods of Blean and Harethum, covers
something like a third of the kingdom. Supplemented by
tracts of marsh pasture in the low lands of the Thames and
Stour, and in Romney Level, Walland, and Oxney, it feeds
the herds of the king, the freeman, and the noble. The most
northerly manor will have its member far to the south in the
Weald. The farthest inland will have its salt marshes upon
the coast.

Thus there is a triplicity of composition, the agricultural
core, the woodland, and the marsh, in these great south-
eastern estates, which comes from the custom of the original
settlers, and persists as a distinctive characteristic throughout
the Middle Ages. As sometime capital of the lathe, Wye
possessed an ample share in these national pastures. Almost
the whole of the modern parishes of Cranbrook and Hawkhurst and much of that of Biddenden were taken up by the
denes or forest walks of the Abbot. The whole was a forest
pasture divided by half the breadth of the county from the
parent manor. Its marsh lay at an almost equal distance
in the salterns about Lydd and Dengemarsh. These had
belonged to Wye from time immemorial.[2]

---

[1] In the parishes of Cranbrook, Hawkhurst, Biddenden, Halden, Woodchurch,
Bethersden, and Pluckley. P.R.O. Excheq. Augm. Off. M.B. 56, ff. 184–205.

[2] *Cart. Sax.* 214: 'Terra regis aduui ubi nominant denge mersc' (A.D. 774).

But this is not all that the map has to tell. No less than the pasture the central, agricultural mass of such a manor as Wye has been moulded into an unfamiliar form by custom. Here we are in the hidated land of the lathe, where the plough has run from time beyond memory, and where the peasant community has preserved the primitive integration of the Kentish folk. We receive the impression of a loosely organized society, a diffused population, a decentralized agriculture.

The virgates of the Midland manor are ideal rather than real. As coherent masses of land they have no existence. Demesne is mixed with tenant land. Nevertheless, scattered as they are, three fields and a single township contain them all. With the tenements of these Kentish estates the reverse is true. In Kent, each tenement is a single and coherent whole, not a partner in a village association nor sharing in its fields, but an agrarian settlement in itself, often miles away from its neighbours or from the central hall of the manor, and the lord's land is also in severalty. Fragments of the demesne and inland of Wye occur sporadically in four hundreds and some twenty parishes; something of the scattering is due to this. But for the most part these detached limbs are peasant tenements. The *terra villanorum* which is contracted within the ring-fence of the Midland village is here an archipelago of hamlets. Not one square mile of land, but fifty, would be necessary to comprise the area of woodland, hill, and valley within which we might come upon some group of tenants by the manor's custom, cut off from their fellows, surrounded by the lands of other lordships, and working their fields in isolation and by their own resources. Each is a yoke, a *jugum*,[1] held by the manor's common custom of gavelkind, assessed to rent and service, owing suit to the manor court. Together they make up the geldable land upon which the Domesday assessment falls. In the common English of the shire they are called the *outland*, while the lord's fields, scattered and in severalty like the tenant's, are called the *inland* when let to tenants, *demesne* when held *in manu domini*.

The tenements of Wye are thus dependent islands,

[1] 1 sulung = 4 juga.

surviving to-day as farmsteads. They occur at intervals spread over the modern parishes of Wye, Boughton Alulf, Godmersham, Crondall, Brook, Willesborough, Ashford, Kingsnothe, Sevington, and Orlestone, not in one unbroken expanse or gathered into *culturae*, but interspersed among the lands of other tenants-in-chief, each a rounded hamlet complete in its own fields and sufficient to itself. Sometimes we shall find two or three juga grouped together, and with a certain amount of intermixture of their tenure, but more often a single jugum or a fraction will maintain a separate and independent life. The area over which they are scattered is some 9 miles by 4, from the church of Challock on the west to the border of the township of Wye on the east, and north and south from the northern border of Wye to Orlestone. Beginning from the north is the single yoke of Kingswood, and next to it, but separate by a mile of woodland, the two juga of the hamlet of Bilting. Another mile and we come to the two juga of Crundale. These, with Perry Nel and Richard, form a northern group, widely separated from each other, and divided from the southern group by the whole extent of the parish of Wye. Crossing this we come by way of Wilmington, through Boughton Alulf parish, to Nackholt, two miles away, and Plumpton, on the Brabourne border. Finally, in scattered isolation, come the four yokes of Ashurst, the yoke of Sevington, and the half yoke of Orlestone.

Examples of this economy could be drawn from almost any manor from which the names of the tenements have come down to us. In the lathe of Eastry, Norborne held substantial tenures in twelve parishes of the hundred of Cornilo. Its 18 sulungs were islands of outland surrounded by an inextricable patchwork of inland, demesne, knight's fees, and free-tenures, manors of the baronies of Say, Badlesmere, and Avranches, and lands of other churches, the priory of Langdon, the Domus Dei of Dover, and the Canons of St. Martin. The sulungs of Tickenhurst, Sutton, and Ripple lay in the parishes of those names, Finglesham and Bettishanger in the north and centre of the main portion of Norborne, West Studdal, Ashley, Minacre, and Napchester in a detached enclave of that parish to the south.

East Studdal lay in Little Mongeham parish, Winkland in Sutton, Martin in East Langdon. In all this Norborne is typical. Littlebourne,[1] Eastrey,[2] Adisham,[3] Chislet,[4] Ickham,[5] all tell the same tale of dispersed and isolated tenements bound into an artificial unity for the gafol and service and suit of the manor, and these tenements are the ancient customary holdings of the peasantry, and testify to the ancient form of the settlement.[6]

Such is the ground-plan of the Kentish manor, a central hall, an archipelago of islands of demesne, inland, and outland, blocks of pasture in the southern forest belt, marsh pasture upon the Thames, Stour, or Romney. Its unity is clearly fiscal and jurisdictional and nothing more. Its tenements lie remote from the curia and from each other, and there is no trace of the Midland common fields.

And yet there is a scheme underlying the Kentish settlement. The scattering of the tenements is more than a negation of the village. The Kentish system, like that of the Midlands, is the outcome of an organic national life, the life of a free peasantry, hamlet dwellers *ut fons, ut campus, ut nemus placuit.* It is natural to think of this as a hamlet system in contrast to the village, and there is contemporary warrant for doing so,[7] yet in using the term at all we beg questions which are vital to the inquiry. If these tenements are indeed hamlets they should possess certain positive features. We ought not to use the term of a casual gathering of population, or of one which has no independent life of its own. By

---

[1] *Black Book of St. Augustine*, ed. G. J. Turner and H. E. Salter, i. 197 (hereafter quoted as *B.B.*).

[2] Library of the Dean and Chapter of Canterbury. Reg. J, f. 31 b.

[3] Ibid., f. 39 a.   [4] *B.B.* ii. 105.

[5] B.M. Add. MS. 6159, f. 32 a.

[6] These manors lie in east and central Kent: from the south we have Bilsington in Lymenewara Lathe (B.M. Add. MS. 37018, f. 42 a), lying in nine parishes, Bilsington, Newchurch, St. Mary, Eastbridge, Snargate, the Romney Marsh, Kingsnorth, Willesborough, and Ruckinge; from the Lathe of Aylesford, Meopham, inland juga distributed over 4 miles by 2½ (B.M. Add. MS. 1006, f. 88 a); from the Lathe of Sutton-Dartford; Dartford and Sutton, Wilmington, Gilde, Stone Hill, Portbridge, Bicknor, Grandisons, Combe, Chislehurst, Cranstead, and Row Hill (P.R.O. *Inq. p.m.* C. Edw. I, File 71 (22)). Otford (B.M. Add. MS. 902, f. 68 a).

[7] Bodl. MSS., Tanner, 240, f. 40 b: 'Wingham cum omnibus hamelettis suis'; *Book of Fees*, i. 623: 'Queruntur quod . . . non venerunt omnes ad curiam que vocatur lagheday . . . nisi tantum duo homines de singulis hamelettis.'

the hamlet we should mean a settlement which has known and fixed bounds. It need not lie within the circle of a single fence, but it must be self-contained, with little or no mingling with the land of its neighbours. It should, in short, be in itself an agrarian unit. It should also be an agricultural unit. It should contain enough arable land to employ its cultivators, and such easements of wood and pasture as are necessary to the course of agriculture, and these easements should be held in severalty. Only then can we accept the hamlet as something more than an offshoot, or the result of the breakdown of some larger agricultural scheme. It must be self-determining, self-sufficing, if it is to be thought of as the basis of a whole society.

All these signs of an organic system are present in Kent. Seen at close quarters, the sulungs and juga reveal themselves as completely organized economic units. Their dependence upon a manorial centre in Norman times, or on a *villa regis* before the Conquest, was a purely external one for rent and jurisdiction and inconsiderable customs of labour. It bore no relation to the tenants' needs in cultivation. There was a real severalty in the soil of the tenements. The sulung lay apart. It contained all the resources of wood and waste which its cultivation required, its several meadow, its wood pasture in Andred for the swine, its several wood within the hamlet, its salt pastures in the marshes for the sheep, and it contained them within carefully delimited boundaries, which seem to have remained unchanged for an indefinite number of centuries.

First as to the unity of the tenement. Upon the fringe of the hamlet area of Sussex, hamlet and village lie side by side as persistent in their difference as the English and Welsh villages of a Marcher lordship. In such conditions the surveyor is bound to point the contrast and to find definitions which shall make clear the status, rights, and duties of these two peasant stocks which find themselves so oddly juxtaposed in the pages of a single survey. A terrier of Battle deals with two groups of Sussex estates to the east of Lewes. They are upon the border of the provinces of the unitary and federative manors. In one group is Alciston. It is unitary in the Midland form, from the foundation of the three open fields to the heavy service paid to the Abbot. Its neighbour, Buckstepe in the parish of Warbleton, is equally plainly Kentish in its scattered tenements and its lighter service. The two lie within 5 miles of each other, but the formulae of description used in the survey separate them by the whole gamut of custom. The virgates of Alciston, says the surveyor, *jacent divisim in lez Comynfeldes*, and shows them equally divided in strips between the three great fields or *leynes* into which the village of Alciston falls, according to the Midland rule.[1] At Buckstepe, in obvious contrast, each tenement has its name.[2] Being a coherent plat of land, each is denoted by the tracing of its encircling bounds, and since the loose articulation of the manor has spread itself over several parishes, the name of every tenement, its bounds, the parish within which it falls, must all be recorded before the land in question is adequately described. The typical formula of record is, therefore, *tenementum de X, in parochia de Y, per metas et bundas subscriptas*, the bounds from point to point following the name of every tenement.[3] The whole contrast of structure stands out boldly in these neighbouring estates; at Alciston the 3 common fields in which the 50 or 60 strips of the virgate are ranged in orderly rotation, and for the most part in the hands of a single tenant; at Buckstepe, the undivided tenements, named, since they are real and familiar units of the countryside, each an unbroken whole lying within its measured boundaries, but shared by many *socii*.[4]

We might assume, perhaps, the antiquity of this severalty. Systems of custom are not changed by art. But good fortune has preserved for us a group of original charters which establishes an identical field system in the second decade of the ninth century. Between the years 811 and 815 Cenwulf,

[1] P.R.O. Excheq. Augm. Off. M.B. 56, f. 246 b.   [2] Ibid., f. 15 a.

[3] Ibid., f. 1: 'Johannes Ludlegh, Simon Watte et socii sui tenent diversas terras et tenementa de tenura virgate terre vocate Ludleghisyerd, que quidem virgata jacet in parochia de Bekle in hundredo de Bello et in burgo de Glaseye per metas et bundas subscriptas.'

[4] So also: *Bilsington*: 'Dola Godewini jacet . . . inter feodum Sacristie Ecclesie Christi Cantuarie et dolam Mawgeri et capitat ex parte australi ad regiam stratam que ducit a Cruce Johannis Cobbe usque Northene. Et predicta dola continet xl acras terre jacentes conjunctim.' B.M. Add. MS. 37018, f. 42 a.

Gillingham: 'Jugum Foghell', &c. Add. MS. 33902.

king of Mercia, was breaking up the north-eastern portion
of the lathe of Faversham,[1] and made a succession of sales to
Wulfred, then Archbishop of Canterbury, who took care to
preserve at Canterbury the original charters which we possess
to-day. The lands are conveyed in four charters detailing
the sulungs, Suiðhunincg lond,[2] æt Grafon eah,[3] Cynincges
cua lond,[4] and Seleberhting lond,[5] and show clearly that the
outlines of the medieval tenement are not the result of later
enclosure. The tenements are *in regione suburbana ad
oppidum regis*, 'in the outland of the king's vill', and are thus
parcels of the estate of Faversham, like the hamlets of Wye,
assessment units from which gafol and service are due.
Here in ninth-century Kent, like his successors 600 years
later, the peasant has shunned the community of his fellows.
The 4 sulungs of Cenwulf's charters are ranged one beside
the other, each bordering, but not encroaching, upon its
neighbour. The sulung æt Grafon eah, the Graveney of
Domesday[6] and to-day, lies along the southern shore of the
estuary of the Swale; to the west it marches with Seleberht's
heirs across the Ealhfleot; its other frontiers are conter-
minous with sulungs bounded like itself.[7] This is the terrier
of a great royal estate in the days before the Saxon conquest,
and the lowest stratum of the field system of the peasantry
has hardly changed when we see it again in Angevin
England.

The Kentish tenement, therefore, satisfies our first test of
individuality. It is an agrarian unit. It is an agricultural
unit also. The hamlet was no casual grouping of the land
of neighbours, but an agricultural whole, informed by the
life and activity of a closely organized body of cultivators.
The character of the Midland co-operative village is best
seen in the disposition of its arable land, and the essential
feature of this is its regular dispersal in two or three fields.
With whatever variations, this open-field system is an

[1] *Cart. Sax.* 335: 'In regione suburbana ad oppidum regis . . . Fefres hám;'
ibid. 353: 'In regione qui dicitur Febres ham.'
[2] Ibid. 335.   [3] Ibid. 341.   [4] Ibid. 348.   [5] Ibid. 353.
[6] D.B. i. 4 a: 'Gravenel. Pro uno solin se defendit.'
[7] *Cart. Sax.* 341: 'Ab aquilone habens terminum Suuealuue fluminis. A plaga
oriente Suithuning lond, a parte occidentali ealhfleot. Ab austro Sighearding
meduue ond eac Suithhuning long.'

organic order, which responds not only to the needs of cultivation, but to the complex of rights and relations which make up the custom of the folk and the manor. An examination of the arable land of the south-eastern hamlet shows that it too reflects an equally definite social scheme, though one of a very different nature, and that while the three-field village is conditioned by the blend of precarious individual right with the servitude of villeinage, the hamlet expresses in a single-field system the opposite qualities, freehold right, tempered by the close association of a peasant group which is primarily a group of co-heirs.

The clearest possible proof of the unity of these peasant groups is found in the primitive form of the ploughland as a single common field, a 'great field', and this has persisted into the Middle Ages. At Bilting[1] the half jugum 'de Crulle' has only one considerable area of ploughland, a plat of $31\frac{1}{2}$ acres. Four tenants share it, but it is a single *campus*, called by the name of the jugum, 'Crulleffeld'. At Wye[2] the principal arable field of the jugum 'de Chilcheborne' is known as 'Chilcheborneffeld', though there are a number of smaller enclosures. At Newchurch,[3] though some of the *dolae* are split into closes and smaller fields by partition, others, as for instance the half dola Mawgeri, retain the single campus, the land of the individual tenants being localized in it by some such phrase as *jacens juxta terram Godwini ex parte australi*. This single field is the *gretefeld* of the Wye *juga*, the main arable mass which figures in the vernacular as the *land* in contrast with the *tun* or houseplace, the *hamme* or meadow, the *teagh* or close, and the *den* or forest pasture of the Weald. In charters of the ninth century, as where the sulungs of Faversham are described in their several parts of Seleberhtinglond, Sighearding medwe,[4] and the like, the *land* appears as a term of technical usage, the *great-field* of arable in contrast to the meadow, wood, or marsh, and gives its name to the sulung.

The prevalence of the single field points to the hamlet

---

[1] P.R.O. Excheq. Augm. Off. M.B. 56, f. 123 a.

[2] Ibid., f. 112 a. So in the jugum de Forda, the largest field, 17 acres, is Fordefelde, the rest being mainly in 'brokelondes', i.e. assarts, gardens, crofts, &c. Ibid., f. 123 b.   [3] B.M. Add. MS. 37018, f. 44.   [4] *Cart. Sax.* 353, 341.

tenement as the sole effective economic group. We have still, however, to consider whether it was entirely independent and its severalty complete in soil other than ploughland. It is possible to imagine a system in which the arable land lay in detached blocks of freehold, but in which all the pasture was the property of a lord as manorial waste. Under such conditions the plough would not be self-supporting. For the pasture of the plough-team, and for dairy and sheep farming, the tenant would still be at the mercy of a lord and involved in the machinery of a larger agricultural community, and it is a general rule of medieval economics that in proportion as the individual tenant is committed to seigneurial monopoly, the freedom of his tenure and person tends to lose its completeness. Surveys and charters are explicit, and make it clear beyond doubt that the peasant tenement of Kent had in free severalty all those easements which the Saxon virgate had precariously and in common. We shall not expect much uniformity in this. Nothing like a normal equipment of wood, grassland, and marsh can be laid down: the proportion will vary from tenement to tenement and from district to district. Kent is too diverse to permit of generalization.

Abbot Ludlow's survey of the lands of Battle Abbey is typical of central Kent. The manor of Wye lies on the higher land between the waters of the Stour and Rother. Half-way between the Weald and the Marsh, it is an open, downland country, broken by woods and by streams which flow north and south from the low watershed. The jugum de Cucklescombe lay on the southern edge of Wye parish, 187 acres in the name of a single owner, John de Oarde. The messuage itself lay in a shallow valley between the rising grounds of the West Down and the Tilth Hill, and about it lay the arable land of the hamlet. Beyond the Tilth Hill and above it, the land rose to the open downs, and here Cucklescombe had its pasture, *c acras pasturae in la Playne super montem.*[1] Along this ridge a succession of juga were alined, and behind the down was portioned off as the

---

[1] P.R.O. Excheq. Augm. Off. M.B. 56, f. 110: 'Johannes de Oarde tenet totum predictum jugum, videlicet super West Doune xx acras. Item in curtilagio de Cockelescombe et in valle ejusdem inter Longhestrete et Tilthehelle xij acras. Item

several pasture of each jugum, taking its name at that point
from the tenement, so that 'Cokelescombedoune' gives place
to the 'Mons de Waleweye' at the point where the hills pass
within the bounds of the neighbouring jugum de Waleweye.[1]
The juga were equally well provided with woodland,
whether in the denes of the Weald, in woods at Wye in a
compact mass or, as in some other manors, lying in small
areas of severalty attached to each tenement. In the detached
section of the parish of Wye which lies to the north-west was
the Kingswood, in which each of the *juga servilia* had 10
acres without rent or service[2]—not the mere right of *husbote*
which is part of the Midland common, but a freehold which
carried with it the right to fell timber, and to fence the 10
acres as a several holding.[3] The free juga, of course, had
their wood-right in the Weald.[4] The Wye tenements,
therefore, seem to have been amply provided with such
pastures as the country afforded and to have held them in
severalty.

Upon the coastal plain by Thames, Stour, and Romney,
the gavelkind pasture is principally marsh, and the jugum
and sulung take a dual form from the very necessity of the
case—on the one hand is the ploughland upon the *terra arida*
above sea-level, and on the other the *terra marisci*, at or below
the tide-mark. Here the juga have marsh pasture in severalty,
but often at some distance from the matrix of arable. By a
grant of the early thirteenth century the Abbot of Saint
Augustine conveyed to one Sampson de Guestling a sixth
part of a jugum in gavelkind as of the manor of Snaves *cum
marisco ad eam pertinente*.[5] The jugum lay in two blocks, one,

in Ladycrofte ij acras. Item super Tilthehelle xl acras. Item in la Playne super
montem c acras pasturae.'

[1] At Meopham, in west Kent, the jugum of Boughurst is backed by Boughurst
Wood and Boughurst Down, Broomfield by Broomfield Down, and so on as at Wye.

[2] *Custumals of Battle Abbey*, p. 133: 'Jugum apud Beudrege habens x acras de
bosco sine redditu.'

[3] In contrast to the socage tenures 'que non possunt prostrare maremium crescens
in tenementis que tenent sine licencia.' P.R.O. Excheq. Augm. Off. M.B. 57, f. 21 a.

[4] P.R.O. Excheq. Augm. Off. M.B. 56: 'Henwode . . . hoc jugum . . . habet . . .
boscum in Wallis.' *Custumals of Battle Abbey*, p. 132: 'Henwode . . . habet dennam
suam per se.' D.B. i. 12 b (Wye): 'Ralf de Curbespine, tenet unam denam et unum
jugum de terra sochmannorum.'

[5] *B.B.* ii. 460: ibid. i. 95 (Chislet): 'Tenentes istarum sulingarum . . . quicunque
habet terram in marisco tenetur facere wallam contra mare.'

which must have been arable, abutting on the churchyard of
the parish of Stone, while the other, the marshland, *contra
sudsexam terminatur*.

The evidence for several pasture in the Middle Ages lies
in every survey and charter.[1] Naturally enough, there is
nothing like the same volume available for the period before
the Conquest, and we are confined to charters which, as a
rule, convey whole groups of sulungs without regard to their
individual composition. A series of the ninth century grants
land in and about Rochester and Lyminge, with appendant
marsh. If we can trust the early Norman period in this
matter it would have been originally held in gavelkind.[2] A
second series is that which I have already used to prove the
severalty of the sulungs of Faversham. The formulae of
pasture grant which are embodied in almost all English
charters have been regarded as no more than common form,
legal phrases rather than descriptions of actual pasture. In
general the Kentish charters are exceptions to this rule in so
far as it is well founded. They have an individuality which
carries conviction that they are meant to be descriptive of
woods, fields, and marshes as they actually lay, and the
pasture which they profess to give can often be traced by
name in the surveys of the Middle Ages. When, therefore,
we find that Cenwulf's grants at Faversham—almost certainly of gavelkind land—convey marshland in accurate
descriptive terms, we may be fairly sure that the conveyance
was more than a form of words necessary to preserve the
traditional form of grant. *Terra quoque duorum aratrum in
locis nominatis thæt Suithuning lond, æt Grafon aea . . . cum
campis pascuis pratibus silvis saltibus piscuosis ac maritimis
fretibus paludibus vallibusque dulcis salsugines coctionesque et
cum cunctis fructibus interius exteriusque vel aliunde usquam ad
eas rite pertinentia.* In this confused and barbarous jumble

----

[1] Cf. the *Inquisitiones post mortem*, Feet of Fines, and the charters printed in the
Black Book, *passim*.

[2] *Cart. Sax.* 486: 'An haga in meridie castelli Hrobi et decem jugera . . . et
communionem marisci quae ad illam villam antiquitus cum recto pertinebat';
ibid. 502: '80 acres "et unum viculum dimidium civitatis Hrobi et unum mariscum
quae ad illum pertinet" ' (A.D. 860 and 862); ibid. 341: 'in regione on Liminum . . . an ioclet ad id insuper addito illo litore foris maritimo in regione on
Liminum.'

of easements, no one can fail to detect a deliberate attempt
to include all the values of a marshy sea-board, careless of
the rigid formalism of law Latin.

Thus the severalty of the Kentish tenements is complete,
and shows no sign of becoming less so as we bring in evidence the few charters of earlier centuries which reveal the
structure of individual sulungs and juga. Not only do they
avoid the commitment of their arable land in the common
field of a village, but their ploughing is backed by a full
ownership in severalty with all those easements of wood,
marsh, and meadow which are necessary to support the
plough-team and the household of the cultivator. They are
agricultural groups perfectly formed after their kind, and
have as complete an equipment for the course of agriculture
as the village has in the Midlands. *Tenementum cum camera
de petra superedificata cum gardino, cum boscis, planis, pascuis
et omnibus pertinenciis*[1], a description of one of the *juga* of
Lenham, is a record which may stand for all.

Underlying the manor, therefore, we find a community
of independent hamlets, each group of cultivators converging
upon its single field of arable, and farming it with its own
resources of wood and pasture. It is in this sense that I call
the Kentish estates federative, and such are the manors of
large areas elsewhere in the south-east, seen in their agrarian
plan upon a single plane; a central hall, an archipelago of
demesne, inland and outland, forest members in the southern
Weald, marshes on the Thames, the Stour, or Romney; a
fiscal and jurisdictional federation, but not a unity for tillage.
Of the Midland common field there is no trace. All this
loosely composed fabric of lands falls under three kinds of
tenure, the *outland*, the *inland*, and the *demesne*. The
demesne is the land *in manu domini*, tilled by his own ploughs
and for his own profit. The inland is like the tenant land,
the *terra villanorum*, of the Midlands. The ultimate land-
right in the inland is the lord's, but it is given over to customary tenures of immemorial antiquity held by sokemen,
cotarii, and the like. These tenants, *inmanni* is the inclu-
sive Kentish term for them, have no writ of defence, but
their expulsion, except for defect of service, would be an

1 *B.B.* ii. 490.

impossible outrage upon custom. Inland and demesne together make up an estate which is equivalent in its tenurial elements to the manor, *terra in dominio* and *terra villanorum*, of the Midlands, though it lies in severalty and scattered. Beyond them, moving in a sphere of quasi-independence unknown in the Midlands, is the outland, the land of the Kentish peasantry *par excellence*, where the lord has no right of property, and tenure is by gavelkind, the ancient custom of Kent. The clearest way to express the difference between the Midlands and the south-east in this matter is to say that while the mass of peasant tenure is within the fee, within the land-right of the lord, in the Midlands, here it is outside it, and held by the lord only *in servitio*. For this, among other reasons, the usages of the Kentish peasantry of the outland have an unusual power of resistance to seigneurial influence. In the custom of the outland we have the ancient folk-right of Kent not greatly changed, and in it, mixed with smaller matters, we may come across the foundations of Kentish government.

The time spent in examining the build of these great estates is not wasted, for the plainest way of approach to a primitive society is through the agrarian ground-plan. If it were granted, and I do not think it should be, that the intricate internal accommodation of champion farming, village community, and manorial lordship was no more than an inevitable adjustment to a countryside of impermeable surface, and hamlet settlement the invariable response where the surface can easily be pierced for water, we should still be faced with the intimate relation of rural economy to law and custom and social relations. The custom that will serve a populous village will not govern a countryside of hamlets, and government, by immediate sympathy or the slow attrition of time, will adjust itself to the humble but obstinate custom of the folk it governs. With this in mind, we may safely take the step upward from fields and homesteads to the folk who tilled and lived in them. The Kentish hamlet is more than the soil it grows upon; it is a group of cultivators. Their relation to each other and to the larger community of which they form a part will in some measure be determined by those material conditions of life that we have been con-

sidering, but we shall find that while much of the custom of
the hamlet arises from the peculiar independence and isolation in which it possesses the soil, the hamlet community,
in its turn, imposes the stamp of peasant freedom upon the
provincial units of which it forms an immediate part, and
that these in turn govern the freest of the English nations.
The hamlet, in fact, and not the manor, is the microcosm of
Kentish life.

(b) THE CUSTOM OF KENT

We have seen that the constituent unit of Kentish life was
not the manor, but the hamlet. In the present section I wish
to emphasize certain qualities in the life and custom of the
dwellers in these hamlets which seem to me to lift them out of
the category of manorial peasantry and prove them to have
enjoyed the full and free custom of a primitive Teutonic
folk, for Kentish peasant custom has elements which show
that it had its origin not in manorial usage but in provincial
law. Chief among these elements are the sanctity of the
birthright and the consequent predominance of the kin,
fundamental independence of seigneurial authority, freedom
of status, and freedom from predial service.

First, as to the kindred. The most striking feature of
Kentish peasant custom in the Middle Ages, gavelkind, is
extreme individualism and the division of the tenement into
separate holdings among each generation of heirs. *Que si
ascun tenant en gavylekende murt . . . que touz ses fitz partent cel
heritage per ouele porcioun*, is the provision of the *Constitutiones*,
and the remedies provided by the common law, taken as a
whole, assume that partition was the normal usage; 'partibility
is the primary and more eminent quality of gavelkind'. The
ownership of the tenant is absolute. If he die intestate the
ancient rule of partible inheritance will take effect, but during
his lifetime there is an absolute discretion in him to change
its course: he may sell it, give it, or devise it, so that
the heritage of his heirs by custom may never mature and the
last vestige of family right may be extinguished. The
authority of the kindred, which was strong enough among
the Celts, and perhaps among the Franks, to keep the lands
of the family together for four generations, and then to

impose an equal redistribution among all the male heirs of its founder, is here a mere shadow of its former self, riddled by the growth of individualism and the individual's right to dispose of his own.

All this has a modern air. But admitting that division was the rule of thirteenth-century law, it is difficult to believe that it held the field in practice. It is likely that the extreme individualism which split the average tenement into scores of holdings was to some extent unreal. Some degree of co-operation, regular or informal, must have been resorted to by the gavelkind tenants if their land was to reach anything like its potential output, and, even as late as the reign of Edward I, there are signs that co-operation rather than individualism has been the rule of the past.

For what it is worth, the nomenclature of the hidation suggests a primitive association between the hamlet and the joint plough. The unit is the sulung and its quarter is the yoke, the jugum of two oxen. At least one ninth-century reference shows sulung and eight-ox plough going together,[1] and the identity was often real even at the end of the thirteenth century, though the great plough had sometimes given way to a lighter four-horse team. Domesday confuses a record which might have been invaluable by combining the teams of the *villani* and *bordarii* in a single total. By making an allowance of 25 per cent. for the ploughs of the bordars— perhaps the tenants of the inland were meant by this—we arrive at a rough equation of one plough to each jugum in the four western lathes, and of rather more than one plough to each sulung in St. Augustine's and Eastrey. No weight could be placed upon this were it not that the equivalence seems to be with the real tenement of the fields, the hamlet, for it allows for the substitution of the jugum for the sulung as the fiscal and servicial unit of private account in the west.[2] Two hundred years later the rule of one plough for the hamlet is still roughly observed, and the scribes of Christ-

[1] Seebohm, *English Village Community*, p. 139, quoting from MS. Cotton Augustus, ii. 64: 'an half suulung . . . to ðem londe iiij oxan.'

[2] In Domesday the assessment is by sulungs throughout Kent. In west Kent, however, the jugum is the normal unit of the manorial economy, though the real as opposed to the assessed acreage of the tenements does not differ very greatly in the two districts.

church occasionally make use of the *caruca* to denote the tenement.[1] The thirteenth-century customary of the Bishop of Rochester[2] gives us a direct statement of the number of ploughs owned by his *rustici*. At Wouldham 6½ juga have each a single plough. At Frindsbury there are 28 ploughs to the same number of juga, at Southfleet 19 to 25 juga. Less directly, by an analysis of the record of oxyeve, gerserthe, and so forth on the Christchurch estates, we can discover the usage in a part at least of east Kent. At Adisham and Staple[3] 7 sulungs have each a single plough, and the same holds good at Monkton and Eastrey. At Ickham, on the other hand, there are 7 ploughs to 4 sulungs.[4] The rule of one plough one ploughland seems therefore to have been general,[5] though not absolute, and the primitive identification of the tenement with the *aratrum* has still some reality 600 years after its first appearance in the charters.

The relation of the joint plough to a system of partible tenure which has already produced a great deal of subdivision at the time of which we are speaking is a little difficult to visualize. If the tenements were really parcelled among as many tenants as the rentals say they were,[6] not only would the ploughing be extraordinarily complicated, but the sharing of the team and its upkeep would be impossible. Yet the records are clear that the plough was a joint-stock enterprise. The fact is, I think, that we must abandon any attempt to interpret the evidence in the way in which it was convenient for the officials of the estates to set it down, and fall back upon the belief that the realities of peasant life were far more primitive than the system of manorial account by which it was exploited or the common law by which it was explained, and by primitive I mean far more bound by the tie of kindred than by thirteenth-century legalism.

[1] Library of the Dean and Chapter of Canterbury, Reg. C, f. 15 a: 'Redditus et servicia de carruca de Gare, cc acrae;' ibid., f. 16 b: 'Swling de Gare.'

[2] Thorpe, *Custumale Roffense*, p. 1 et seq.

[3] Library of the Dean and Chapter of Canterbury, Reg. J, f. 37 b: 'De consuetudine arandi vij acras de gerserthe in hyeme de Adisham et Staple cum cibo de vij carucis conjunctis vij. sol.'   [4] B.M. Add. MS. 6159, f. 32 a.

[5] P.R.O. Excheq. Augm. Off. M.B. 56, f. 39. At Limpsfield the tenement must plough an acre 'si habuerit unam carucam ut plures in tenemento de Limenenefeld'.

[6] Upon 1 sulung of St. Augustine's tenure there were 40 tenants and groups of tenants to 160 acres.

By the thirteenth century the law has come to lay the strongest emphasis upon the partibility of gavelkind, and to lend its authority to the increasing practice of partition. And yet, in spite of the rule of the courts, it is difficult to believe that division is its radical principle. That it was the law is certain, that it was also custom is by no means so clear, for there were many elements in the custom of tenure which could not be enforced in the courts of the realm. It may, indeed, be doubted whether the lawyers of the early Angevin kings were equipped to deal with such vestiges of joint-family tenure as may have survived in gavelkind. To recognize and enforce the common property of a group of co-heirs presented much the same problem as was then coming to the fore in the boroughs. Was the governing body of the burgesses a corporation capable of holding land as such? The thirteenth century could give no clear answer, for even Bracton had but a hazy notion of corporate ownership, and Bracton's predecessors would have been neither interested nor competent to devise a writ for peasants defending their tenure jointly. We must wait for Littleton for a clear rule of tenure in common. If we find the individual possessed of the field of law, and partition the rule, one reason may well be that the individual's rights and duties absorbed the legal knowledge and imagination of the age.

For this reason the verdict of the plea rolls need not be final. If they are decisive for partition, there is much in custumals and charters to make us think that the hold of the kindred upon its land was too tenacious to sanction an invariable rule of partition. Even so late as the fifteenth century the lists of single tenures are broken by an occasional entry of tenure by groups of heirs: *Heredes Thome Baker tenent de predicta dimidia dola v acras terre et tres partes unius acre.*[1] Such entries, at so late a period, are the exception and several tenure is the rule, but they make up, perhaps, 10–20 per cent. of the whole, and as we go backward in time the proportion and the size of such tenures grow larger, till, in a list which is attributed to the reign of Henry III, half the unfree juga and all but four of the free juga of Wye are recorded as being held each by a single group of co-

[1] B.M. Add. MS. 37018, f. 44.

heirs.[1] Much the same proportion prevailed in the lands of Christchurch and St. Augustine, two-thirds of the land at Lenham being held in the reign of Edward I by groups of *heredes, fratres, socii,* or *pares,*[2] while at Chartham and West-well the ratio was about the same.[3] As we approach the dead line beyond which direct evidence fails us the ties of kindred assert themselves more plainly. In the fifteenth century the officials had to do for the most part with individuals: in the thirteenth with fratres or heredes, socii or pares.

The meaning of these groups of associates is not immediately evident. No doubt they stood as partners in service, but their holdings were quite irregular and often very small, so that the estate was none the better for their grouping.[4] Indeed, those estates which preferred to deal with their tenants in groups kept the whole tenement together and appointed a ministerial representative known as the *suling-man,* who was chosen by his fellow tenants and collected the rents of the sulung as a whole. The manor was, therefore, in a position to ignore the disposition of the soil as between the tenants and to allow matters to work themselves out naturally. On the other hand, the wording of extents suggests that the impulse towards grouping—perhaps it would be more correct to say, the resistance to partition—came from the tenants themselves. Great care is taken to record the nature of the groups of tenants, a matter which would not affect the profit of the estate, but which did concern the holders vitally. Pares, socii, participes, parcenarii, and the like may perhaps be taken as synonyms. Besides these there are fratres and heredes in about equal proportion, with an occasional intermediate relationship, such as the Lenham tenure of *Willelmus de Tenigfold et heredes fratris eius.* Thus

---

[1] P.R.O. Excheq. Augm. Off. M.B. 18, f. 3 a. Cf. also B.M. MS. Harl. 1708, f. 101 b (a list of tenures at Hoo of the reign of King John): 'Adam Berd et participes ipsius tenent duo juga'et dimidiam.'

[2] *B.B.* i. 255.

[3] Library of the Dean and Chapter of Canterbury, Reg. J, ff. 53 a, 65 a.

[4] P.R.O. *Inq. p.m.* C. Edw. I, File 108 (1): 'Item dicunt quod Simon et Johannes de Gatoce et eorum participes, Ricardus Lane et participes sui, Willelmus . . . lesel et parcenarii sui, Willelmus Colt et parcenarii sui, Rogerus Latter et parcenarii sui, Radulfus Aylard et parcenarii sui, Ricardus Heverel et parcenarii sui, Reginaldus de Cobbeham et parcenarii sui, Robertus Gerveys et parcenarii sui arabunt et hercia-bunt xj acras et dimidiam, j rodam et dimidiam rodam.'

the groups sometimes consisted of cousins, and, indeed, *heredes* might be taken to cover relationship known but too complicated to be recorded in a survey, while *pares* might consist of still more remotely connected groups, or of voluntary associations of neighbours for convenience of cultivation. Law will have it that the principle of gavelkind is the division of the heritage among co-heirs: surveys tell us rather of the community of heirs, and such unity served no purposes of their lords. Is it not possible that the peasantry, having sold its birthright for the protection of the law in the only form in which the age could give it, that of several property, may have been incapable of carrying out the bargain, and have continued to conduct its affairs by the rules of immemorial custom, custom controlled by the Teutonic instinct of the kin?

There is a good deal of positive evidence that this was so. The law of gavelkind, though it is in general conceived to meet the needs of a partible tenure, has been forced to provide remedies for cases in which partition has not in fact been carried out. Such are the Writ of Partition, under the Statute of 31 Henry VIII, to enable one coparcener to secure his pourparty against the wish of the others, and the Writ *Insimul Tenuit*, for a purpose similar to *Mort d'Ancestor*, as between the heirs of tenants in common. Gavelkind inheritance has, moreover, this significant resemblance to tenure in common, that for purposes of seisin the entry of one coparcener is the entry of all. Indirectly, therefore, the law does recognize that gavelkind may remain undivided. Again, it is legitimate to question whether group tenures do not lie behind a proportion of those early fines and charters where two or more persons appear as grantors or parties to a final concord. *Sciant presentes et futuri quod ego Willelmus et ego Jocelinus et ego Walterus et ego Reginaldus et ego Ioannes filii Swetman de Bois dedimus . . . Willelmo de Chetherste . . . totam partem terre nostre que nobis contingit . . . que est in campo de Godieveland.*[1] This is one of many group charters which are preserved in the gavelkind records of St. Augustine, and they may be paralleled from the final concords.[2] Some of

[1] *B.B.* ii. 500.
[2] Pedes Finium. 23 May 1204: 5 John. Final concord 'inter Sibillam filiam

these, no doubt, might be explained as the work of immediate coparceners representing the same stock of descent
and alienating the whole of their birthright, but some stand
for real co-operation.[1] Charters granted by larger groups,
moreover, are on a different footing. The seisin of cousins
in the second and third degrees can hardly represent the
same stock of descent if the tenure has been departed at each
generation, nor could their property have resulted from a
single general seisin. We have charters from Lenham which
suggest the persistence of common tenure through at least
four generations, so that the tenement of Colesland was
granted by a group of second cousins, great grandsons of
the original owner.[2] Charters made to groups of persons
also point to common tenure, whether made to brothers or
to recipients in a remoter degree of relationship. Such
charters could establish no separate right in any one of the
grantees to any part of the tenement given, the right of each
being clearly a general common right throughout the whole.

Again, many charters transferring plats of land describe
them as lying between the lands of other tenants, and the
constant mention of *terra heredum* and similar phrases in
these circumstances can only mean that the lands of heirs
were undivided. A common line of demarcation, if it is
used as a mete for neighbouring lands, must mean common
tenure. In this way some of the charters of St. Augustine's
manor of Chislet throw a direct light upon the tenements of
that manor as they stand in the Edwardian survey. Among
the tenants of the *suolinga de Chistelet* in the manor of
Chislet, in the reign of Edward I are the *heredes Hamonis
de Chelde*.[3] A charter of the early twenties of the thirteenth

Radulfi petentem et Johannem et Henricum et Willelmum et Thomam et Petrum
et Elyam et Gaufridum et Gilebertum, filios Alardi Tundu, tenentes, per Radulfum
et Ricardum positos loco suo'.

[1] P.R.O. *Inq. p.m.* C. Edw. I, File 35 (6): 'Predictus Radulfus filius Radulfi
semper pasturabat averia sua propria cum averiis predicti Thome fratris sui et simul
comorabant.'

[2] *B.B.* ii. 480: 'nos Willelmus filius Wyberti de Hamme, Adam, Joannes et
Robertus filii Willelmi de Hamme, Wibertus filius Godwini de Hamme, Mauricius
filius Stephani de Hamme, Walterus et Hugo filii Eylnodi de Hamme, Ricardus,
Adam, Hamo, Mauricius filii Willelmi Francais concessimus . . . totum jus et
clamium quod habuimus . . . in terra de Coleslande.'

[3] *B.B.* i. 105.

century shows one Walter de Goldhavec granting to Ralf
del Blen *totam terram meam . . . in villa de Chistelet, que terra
jacet inter boscum predicti domini Abbatis versus est et terram
heredum Hamonis de Chelde versus west.*[1] The land of the
heirs of Hamon de Chelde, a quarter sulung, was therefore
already a unity in 122–, since it had a common boundary
with its neighbour. It was a unity in an even earlier generation, for the tenants are already the *heredes Hamonis* and we
do not know how far back the eponymous Hamo must be
located. It was still entered as a unity in the survey of
Edward. For at least eighty years then this tenure had been
held in common, and for that indefinite period before the
early thirteenth-century charter which will take us to the unknown date at which Hamo was the living tenant. Within
this period three generations of parceners must have ad-
justed their claims to the changes brought about by death
and birth, but there is no sign of partition. The charter of
122– vouches for the unity of the tenure, the survey vouches
for its unity of service, and in this case at least the proof of
common tenure and joint liability seems to be complete.[2]

Each source of evidence taken alone might, perhaps,
leave us in doubt, but, as a whole, they create a strong
impression that the partible nature of gavelkind has behind
it a history of family solidarity. We cannot venture to put
forward the joint family as existing in theory within historical times, but there is little doubt that it existed in
practice, and it is an allowable conjecture that further evidence from the earliest times would show that the kindred
element was at least no weaker in the past.

The sulung of the later Middle Ages is usually divided
into a number of holdings, some held by co-heirs and some
by individuals, but the sulung name often preserves the
tradition of a time when it was entirely, or largely, in the
hands of a single kindred. In the fifteenth-century survey of
Wye we find tenements known as the *jugum Cnotte, Barde,
Normanni,* and *Geroldi.*[3] They are not the names of con-

---

[1] *B. B.* ii. 405.
[2] Cf. also, Leurenot Sigrun, *B.B.* i, pp. 84, 409; Etard Bedellus, pp. 113, 410;
Ricardus de Marisco, pp. 98, 412; Isaac de Boyton, pp. 93, 412.
[3] P.R.O. Excheq. Augm. off., M.B. 56, f. 110 et seq.

temporary owners, but traditional and of very old standing, the *juga* of the Lancastrian period being split up into numerous several and common holdings. If we turn to the list of the Wye tenements drawn up in the reign of Henry III,[1] we shall find that already, two centuries earlier, the same personal names attach to the *juga*, but now in the form *heredes Geroldi, heredes Normanni, Cnotte*, and *Barde*.[2] Nor must we suppose that an earlier list still would show these eponymous tenants in undivided possession. It is not certain that either Cnotte or Norman ever held the whole of the jugum Cnotte or the jugum Normanni. The full description of their tenants under Henry III is *Cnotte et socii, heredes Normanni et socii*. The earlier the record the more prevailing the influence of the kindred, but the imagined common ancestor recedes before us as we follow him into the past, and if he were ever reached, we should no doubt find that he was no more than the senior of the largest but not the only group of kinsmen within the tenement.

There is a narrow but convincing thread of evidence which carries this usage back to very remote times indeed, for it has behind it an English terminology which can be identified with that of the earliest genuine charters of Kent. The English equivalents of the *terra heredum* during the Middle Ages are formations combining the name of some past tenant with a suffix *-cild*, in the sense of 'heirs'—*Welke-childeland, Webbecildelade*,[3] *Dimidium jugum Foghelchilde*[4]— but, in addition to this, a form with the termination *-ing* occurs, as at Kenardington, where gavelkind lands are held by *quidam homines qui dicuntur Kenewoldinges*,[5] who may well have been the descendants of Kenwold who was a tenant in this manor in 1212, since the name occurs nowhere else among the hundreds of names recorded in the *Black Book*.[6]

How far this termination was in common use after the

---

[1] Ibid. M.B. 18, f. 3 b.

[2] Ibid., M.B. 488, f. 2 a. So also at Ickham. Suling Johannis de la Lee et sociorum eius. Dimidia Suling de Welles quam Eylwin et socii eius tenent. B.M. Add. MS. 6159, f. 33 a.

[3] *B.B.* i. 229, 238.

[4] P.R.O. Excheq. Augm. Off. M.B. 488, f. 1 a. 'Thomas Selbe etc. tenent dimidium jugum Foghelechild pro heredibus de Foghel.'

[5] P.R.O. *Inq. p.m.* C. Edw. I, File 35 (6).

[6] *B.B.* ii. 462.

Norman Conquest we cannot tell. Tenement names formed from those of persons are Latinized in the post-Conquest records, and a vernacular *Wlstaningland* or *Godardingland* for *terra heredum Wlstani* or *Godardi* would, in the nature of our documents, leave no trace, but in pre-Conquest charters this formation plays a great part in Kentish nomenclature. No crux in the history of English place-names has produced more controversy than the interpretation of the suffix *-ing*, and its compounds, none has been made to bear a greater weight of speculation, and it would be a bold amateur who should wake the ghost of Kemble's theory after so many warnings to the curious. It must be admitted that the suffix was sometimes used as a simple genitive or locative, but this use cannot be established before the later half of the ninth century.[1] Its use in the sense of 'son of' had certainly not died out in the tenth century, nor was it confined to poetry or to genealogies of the royal house.[2] But whatever may have been the usage under the Saxon hegemony, there is a flood of instances from the charters of the eighth and early ninth centuries of a use which lifts it out of the traditional line of controversy. Discussion has, perhaps, dwelt most generally upon the bearing which the *-ing* element has upon the origin of units such as the village or the manor, or even larger settlements such as the Faerpingas of the Tribal Hidage. In such cases we are faced by alternative difficulties. If we accept the meaning 'descendants of' we must find room for whole villages bound together by an active sense of kinship; if we believe it to be no more than a possessive form of the personal name we must admit a high degree of manorialism at a very early date indeed. In approaching those Kentish names which include the elements *-ingham*, *-ingtun*, and the like, we must put away from our minds the natural instinct to think of villages or parishes; indeed we must put aside the notion of place-names proper altogether. The names which appear before the Norman Conquest and have won permanent places on the map are few. The common method of the eighth and ninth centuries is to convey single tenements such as sulungs and juga not under a place-name, but under

[1] *Cart. Sax.* 506, Bromleaginga (A.D. 862); ibid. 792 and 814.
[2] Ibid. 576, Eadwald Sibirhtigne; ibid. 1097, Aelfstan Heahstaninc.

that of the tenants, adding to this the name of the lathe or
royal vill in which they lie. *Unum aratrum on Liminum . . . id
est ðæt Pynnhearding lond;*[1] *on Eostorege . . . aratrum . . .
quod Dunwaling lond dicitur,* is the common formula until the
end of the ninth century. Moreover, it is plain that the
suffix *-inglond* is only the centre of a number of subsidiary
formations denoting various parts of the hamlet. Besides
the termination *-ingland,* the arable field, we find *-ingtun,*[2]
the messuage, *-ingham,*[3] the meadow, *-ingden,*[4] *-ingmedwe,*[5]
-ingherst,[6] and others of the same type. *Dunwalingland* is
paralleled by a *Dunwalingden,*[7] which should be the weald
pasture of that tenement, and among the sulungs of the
king's vill of Faversham we find forms such as *-ingmedwe,*
obviously corresponding to the *-ingland* of such units as
Suithuningland and *Seleberhtingland.* It seems clear then that
the suffix *-land* is merely a field-name, that of the principal
field such as is found in Fordfelde or Chilchebornefelde
at Wye, and though this is used as a tenement name for
transferring the holding of which it is the matrix, it has no
permanent validity, but changes as the group of tenants,
Sigheardings or the like, change with the generations and
call themselves from some successor of Sigheard. Unlike the
true place-name, these do not perpetuate themselves upon
the map; and in this they resemble the form *jugum heredum
de X, sulung heredum de Y* which took their place in the
Middle Ages. The suffix *-ing* is associated with small bodies
of land, tenements upon the outland of the royal and comital
estates rather than with such estates themselves. So similar
are these to the patronymics of the Middle Ages in their
personal form and their impermanence that it is natural to
think of them as patronymics also. Nor do I believe that
there is any inherent difficulty in doing so. We should not
be committed to forcing the influence of kindred to the

[1] *Cart. Sax.* 332; ibid. 328, Ealdhuninglond; ibid. 380, Osberhting lond; ibid.
381, Suithberhtinglond; ibid. 449, Deoring lond.

[2] Ibid. 536, Bosingtune.

[3] Ibid. 408, Pleguuiningham.

[4] Ibid. 247, Suið helming daenn; ibid. 442, Hildgaringdenn.

[5] Ibid. 341, Sighearding medwe; ibid. 449, Aling med.

[6] Ibid. 407, Ægelbertinherst.

[7] Ibid. 247 and 332; cf. also Babbingden with Babbing long (for lond), ibid.
316 and 332; Pilfreðincgden with Wlfrethingland, ibid. 396 and 637.

point of incredibility. There need be no question of settlements under patriarchal authority and rigid family communism. We need only admit that the Sigheard or Suithun
of the ninth century was the comparatively recent ancestor
of the largest of the groups in the sulung which bore his
name, as Laurence del Blen or Richard de Stokke were in
the sulungs of Chislet which bore their names for the greater
part of the thirteenth century. In short, we should be committed to no more than the belief that, *ceteris paribus*, the
system of tenement names was the same before the Conquest
as after it.

On the other hand, if we admit these names as patronymics, we cannot but admit that the influence of blood was
stronger at first than it came to be in the Middle Ages, since
they hold the whole field, while after the Conquest territorial
hamlet names first supplemented and later replaced them.
The population was smaller, and it is not unparalleled in
Celtic and Teutonic society that the *pares* of small self-contained hamlets should explain their association upon grounds
of consanguinity. We might expect, too, that real co-operation in agriculture would be more common in primitive
times. The individualism of the thirteenth century was
accompanied by a larger population and extreme partition.
It is less marked as we go back in time. Moreover, the terminology of the hidation suggests that co-operation had been
the rule in the beginning. The *aratrum*, the *sulung*, and its
quarter share, the *yoke*, appear as early as the seventh century,
and can hardly have been entirely unreal. It is possible that
at the back of medieval individualism there may be an
effective association by the whole hamlet for ploughing, and
at least a general belief that the hamlet community was a
group of co-heirs. In these qualities we seem nearer to the
primitive usage of the free Germanic stocks than elsewhere
in England. Our nearest parallel is already with Frankish
kindred organization rather than with the manorialism of
Wessex.

To pass to the second point, freedom. Certainly, the
Kentish gavelkinder was free. The claim is confident and
reiterated, from the earliest plea-rolls to the days of Lambarde and Camden.

'The Yeomanrie, or common people', says Lambarde,[1] 'is no where
more free and jolly then in this shyre, for . . . it is agreed by all men
that there were never any bond-men (or villaines, as the law calleth
them) in Kent. Neither be they here so much bounden to the gentrie
by copyhold or custumarie tenures, as the inhabitants of the westerne
countries of the realme be, nor at all indangered by the feeble holde of
tenant right, as the common people in the northern parts be. But in
place of these, the custome of gavelkind prevailing everywhere, in
manner every man is a freeholder, and hath some part of his own to
live upon. And in this their estate they please themselves and joy
exceedingly.'

Not only did they joy in this estate exceedingly but they
asserted it constantly and with success. There is, indeed, a
kind of Magna Charta, enrolled traditionally before the eyre
of 21 Edward I, the *Constitutiones Cancie*, which embody
all the rules and privileges of gavelkind, and constitute a
recognition of gavelkind custom as the common law of Kent,
and foremost among its claims is the assertion of personal
freedom and freehold: *que toutes les cors de Kenteys seyent
francz; quilz pusent lour terres et lour tenementz donner et
vender saunz conge demaunder*. As soon as we can observe it,
gavelkind has established itself well on the right side of the
uncertain line between free and unfree tenure. Unlike
tenants in all kinds of socage and villeinage, the tenant in
gavelkind sues and is sued in the courts of the eyre.[2]

In the interval between the Norman Conquest and the
stabilization of gavelkind rules by their recognition by the
king's judges there was time for the infiltration of foreign
custom, but the smallness of the change which took place
testifies to the enormous tenacity of local usage. Occasionally
tenures which are clearly gavelkind will be referred to as
villeinage,[3] but villein incidents are few and far between. In
the thirteenth century the churches of Canterbury were
exacting the right of wardship.[4] The Bishop of Rochester

---

[1] *Perambulation of Kent*, p. 7.

[2] Bolland, *Eyre of Kent*, iii. 155; 'Constitutiones Cancie': 'Et que touz e chescun
puseit per bre' le roy, oy per pleynt, pleder pur lour droit purchaser, auxibien de
lour seignerages come des autres gentz.'

[3] *B.B.* i. 6.

[4] *Rot. Hundr.* i. 201: 'Item dicunt quod Archiepiscopus Cantuariensis, Prior
Ecclesie Christi et Abbas Sancti Augustini habent et vendunt maritagia et wardas
sokemannorum aliter quam deberent, quia in Kancia non est warda.'

established the right of pre-emption on the chattels of his tenants in gavelkind, and a modified form of merchet.[1] But these are exceptions, and both explicitly and by their silence the mass of Kentish surveys and inquisitions assert that gavelkind as a whole was free from villein disabilities,[2] and this freedom was asserted point by point in the ancient *Constitutiones Cancie*,[3] while partible inheritance by heirs, and the rights of alienation, dower, and wardship[4] by the kin were everywhere exercised in practice.

The same freedom prevailed in service. Many manors, mostly belonging to the Church, it is true, have a long list of dues to record in the thirteenth century, and there is enough difference from manor to manor to show that local require- ments have hastened their growth. But these differences are in unessentials, and are modern innovations. The true service of gavelkind, that which arises from the nature of the tenure and is general and of proved antiquity, is almost uniform throughout the county. *Gafol, averagia*, with per- haps a boon-work of ploughing and reaping, and the hedging of the lord's demesne, are the universal and ancient services of gavelkind. The king and the lay lords can take no more than this from the men of the outland. Where more is due, it may be traced to the clerical landlord, with his genius for turning free-will offering into obligation.

The 18 sulungs of Monkton in Thanet[5] were traditionally given to the nuns of Thanet in the seventh century, and transferred from them to Christchurch. Towards the end of the thirteenth century the outland rendered as follows: '*Apud Moneketon' sunt xviij swoling' de gavelikende: xvj eorum hec facient servicia per annum. De gablo reddent de qualibet acra*

---

[1] Thorpe, *Custumale Roffense*, p. 2.

[2] P.R.O. *Inq. p.m.* C. Edw. I, File 94 (8) (Aldington): 'Sunt ibidem quidam liberi tenentes de gavelykende.'

[3] 'Que si ascun tenent en gavylekende murt . . . que touz ses fitz partent cel heritage per ovele porcioun.

'Et quilz pusent lour terres et lour tenementz doner et vender, saunz conge demaunder a lour seignerages.

'Et si le heir seit de deins le age de xv ans, seit le nouriture de eux baille al plus procheyn del sank, a qui heritage ne peut descendre.'

[4] P.R.O. Court Rolls, Portf. 181, 74 (Milton): 'Et quia infra etatem sunt ideo . . . mater eorum sequitur pro nutrimento et habet plegios . . . de habenda custodia.'

[5] B.M. Add. MS. 6159, f. 28 a.

jd.ob. Et de mala de quolibet swoling' xx.s. per annum ad iiijor terminos. Et de dono iiijs. De qualibet caruca arabunt unam acram de averherde . . . Et de gadercorn reddunt de quolibet swoling' iiij coppas de puro ordeo. Et de present' gallum et gallinam de quolibet domo ad Natale . . . et ova ad Pascha sicut cuilibet oneratur. Arant preces semel ad conredium curie. De quolibet swoling' duos agnos reddunt in estate. Quod si agnus non inventus fuerit viij.d. dabit quando malam persolvet.'

These services are substantially the same as those of a dozen other manors in the lathes of Eastrey, Saint Augustine, and Sherwinhope, and Monkton may well stand for the type of the ecclesiastical estate. In some the service of *precariae*, in others the *gafol* or *redditus*, may play a slightly larger part, but as a rule there is agreement in essentials and difference only in detail. Not all this is ancient service. It is not difficult to divine that a common principle has been at work to modify and adapt custom to the requirements of a private estate, and, where possible, to exploit it by playing upon the double claim of the saint and the landlord. Yet the elements of gavelkind service are retained with singular fidelity. They are mixed with new customs, some free-will offerings in theory, others forced upon successive generations of tenants by the impalpable pressure of a lordship which never dies and never forgives, but beneath this overlayer of manorial rents and incidents lies the primitive custom of gavelkind. A little consideration will bring it to light.

First, I think, we may set aside the mala or money rent. At Monkton and elsewhere it is the principal constituent of the newer manorial dues. Though common in the church manors, it is not a general incident upon gavelkind. While the outland of the Prior of Christchurch pays mala or firma at Adisham, Godmersham, Westwell, Great Chart, and Mersham, it pays none at Chartham, Brook, Little Chart, and Hollingbourne.[1] The mala is often levied at different rates from different sulungs,[2] and even from different parts

[1] Library of the Dean and Chapter of Canterbury, Reg. J, *passim*. I am much indebted to Mr. W. P. Blore for a transcript of this register.

[2] B.M, Add. MS. 6159, f. 31 a (Eastrey): 'Swling' de Crouthorne viij.s. et vj.d. de mala. Swling' Bismere xij.s. Caldecote de xl acris . . . non dant malam.' Library of the Dean and Chapter of Canterbury, Reg. J. f. 39 a (Adisham):

of the same sulung.[1] It is a variable and exceptional due, for the most part confined to the Abbey lands, and the result of bargains with individual tenants, treated by the tenants as blackmail—*de quolibet sullingo xx.s. mala . . . quos antecessores nostri dederunt pro omnibus injustis et incausacionibus quas vobis ore plenius exponemus.*[2] The main element of rent outside the *gafol* is a modern outcome of the coercion which lordship and the spiritual prestige of the Church can wield.

There are other, smaller renders in which the gavelkind tenants of the church are less well off than their peers under lay tenure, but most of these bear clearly the marks of voluntary gift. The *donum* occurs sporadically. It is a free-will offering; *dominus solebat mittere in illis sulingis servos suos petere in quadragesima et qui volebat dedit prout voluit.* Such begging raids were bought off in many Christchurch manors at a flat rate of four shillings from every tenement. In some they were compounded for by the whole tenantry, inland and outland alike.[3] Such gifts as the lamb at Midsummer, eggs at Easter, poultry at Christmas, and the like,[4] are no more than seasonable offerings, often *de presento* or *de dono*. Rent charges upon the outland therefore, other than the ancient gafol, are not of great antiquity. They may be as old as Domesday, but still they are remembered as exactions.[5]

Freedom from predial service speaks eloquently of freedom of tenure. It is the lawyer's test of villeinage. In this matter, as in so much else, we find that the usages of the south-east are in direct contrast to those of the Midlands.

'Swoling' de Bleding' et Ilding' . . . pro swoling' de mala iiij.s, Swling' de Silveston . . . de mala x.s.'

[1] B.M. Add. MS. 6159, f. 31 a: (Eastrey) 'Item de swling' de Crouthorne unde Walterus reddit de cxxv acris iiij.s.jx.d. Item de eodem swling' terra Radulfi de Crouthorne clxxv acra debet iiij.s.jx.d.' Library of the Dean and Chapter of Canterbury Reg. J, f. 39 a (Adisham): 'Item swling' de Gare est eiusdem servicii preter L acras . . . de quibus non dat malam.' ² *B.B.* i. 60.

[3] Library of the Dean and Chapter of Canterbury, Reg. J, f. 48 a (Chartham): 'De communi dono xx.s.'

[4] B.M. Add. MS. 6159, f. 31 a; Library of the Dean and Chapter of Canterbury, Reg. J, f. 58 a.

[5] The valet of the Canterbury manors, though it appears as a lump sum in the Exchequer Domesday, was in fact divided between *gafol* and *firma*. The Domesday Monachorum of Christchurch renders the 'modo reddit xlvj libras et xvj solidos et iiij denarios' of the Exchequer account of Adisham as 'de gablo reddit xvj libras et xvj solidos et iiij denarios', while the remaining thirty pounds is *firma*. The ancient element *gafol* is thus separated from the newer profits, the *firma*.

In no single manor throughout the county is there the least approach to that week-work by which the demesne of the Midland estates was maintained, nor is there room among the older customary rents for any appreciable body of commutation. Indeed, the reverse is common in Kent. Corn-rents, gafol, carrying services, and other ancient obligations are exchanged for help with the rising industry of demesne farming at ploughing and harvest, and what few opera there are belong chiefly to this new economic phase. At Minster in Thanet, a great manor with a substantial demesne, some of the sulungs pay their gafol in money, some in corn, but some by the service of *gafolerth*, the ploughing, sowing, reaping, and carrying of 2 acres of St. Austin's land;[1] at Chislet[2] the tenants owe the same *de gabulo*; and at Chartham[3] all the gafol has been commuted for various kinds of labour. At the end of the Dark Ages, when money was scarce and demesne farming beginning, the exchange was a fair one for both lord and tenant, and it was widely made.[4] Our records are full of such minor additions and adjustments, and it would be tedious to multiply instances. Nearly all can be traced to some particular feature of demesne farming, and so in a sense to seigneurial influence, but they are, for the most part, confined to the ecclesiastical manors, and even there are heavily outweighed by the staple rent of gafol. Evidently then, many of the light labour dues of Kent arose from modifications of ancient service made necessary by the new economy of the Middle Ages. They have small historical significance and cannot affect our view of the primitive status of gavelkind. When they are cleared away, we are

[1] *B.B.* i. 25.

[2] 'De Sulunga de Fayreport debent arare de gabulo ij acras et herciare et seminare cum semine abbatis.' Ibid. i. 100.

[3] Library of the Dean and Chapter of Canterbury, Reg. J, f. 43 a (Ickham): 'De consuetudine arandi x acras et dimid. de gavelherthe in hyeme'; ibid., f. 48 a (Chartham): 'qui debet arrare i acram de gavelerthe debet metere ij acras et qui debet metere de gavelrip debet ducere ij carectatas.'

[4] P.R.O. *Inq. p.m.* C. Edw. I, File 65 (4): Gavelrip on the lands of John de Peccham at West Peckham; ibid., File 67 (22): on William de Barnelyng's land at Nettlestead; ibid., File 77 (3): on the Clare lands at Brastead; ibid., File 107 (17): Gavelherthe at Boughton Alulf. See also Library of the Dean and Chapter of Canterbury, Reg. J, f. 43 a. Work in return for wood or pasture is rare, since the gavelkinder had his severalty. We find ploughing for geserthe at Adisham and Ickham.

left with a small residuum of service, found in both lay and spiritual tenures, which seem to be precariae in the sense in which that word is understood in other counties.

The commonest kind of boon-work is one which is plainly not an outcome of tenure. It takes the form not of a levy proportionate to the tenement, but of a loan of all the stock of the tenant, who must lend his plough for a day, or plough an acre of the demesne. In neither case does the share of any one tenant depend upon the amount of land he holds, but on the possession of a plough; *de qualibet caruca conjuncta in villa arrare debent j acram*. The service is called *oxyeve*,[1] and is common but by no means universal. It is commonest in the larger manors of the churches of Canterbury, while in small manors, and those of laymen it has disappeared. The Christchurch manors of Ickham,[2] Monkton,[3] Adisham,[4] Little Chart,[5] and Hollingbourne[6] have it; Eastrey, Chartham, Godmersham, Westwell, Great Chart, and Mersham do not.

Precariae assessed on the tenement are hardly more numerous, but they occur in manors held under all kinds of tenure. They include harvest works as well as ploughing. The estate of a single tenant-in-chief may serve to illustrate their distribution. John de Cobham, who died in the twenty-eighth year of Edward I, held the manors of Westchalk, Cobham, Aldington, and Coolinge. In all these he had tenants in gavelkind, and in Aldington he received service of reaping, and of hedging the demesne enclosure.[7] In Westchalk, Cobham, and Coolinge the gavelland was quit for a rent *pro omnibus serviciis*. The instance is typical, and though we may suspect that a certain amount of commutation has taken place, it does not seem that the military tenants could ever depend on their gavelland for more than one or two autumn works, average, and demesne fencing, while many had nothing but gafol. Beyond these light and precarious services Kentish gavelland is free of labour.

---

[1] *B.B.* i. 80: 'Homines de eisdem sulingis . . . debent adiuvare ballivum ad carucas domini quolibet anno, que consuetudo vocatur oxyeve.'

[2] Library of the Dean and Chapter of Canterbury, Reg. J, f. 43 a.

[3] Ibid. 27 b.   [4] Ibid. 37 b.   [5] Ibid. 68 a.   [6] Ibid. 70 a.

[7] P.R.O. *Inq. p.m.* C. Edw. I, File 94 (8): 'Willelmus Enesard et parcenarii eius tenent xx acras terre . . . et metent in autumpno j acram iij rodas bladi.' Cf. also the Honour of Clare, ibid. File 77 (3).

It will be seen that the gavelkind dues reveal a stratification in time. An age later than that of the settlement has deposited a new layer of service, but the primary rock of gavelkind custom is still recognized. It is also marked by a significant limitation of seigneurial power. The manorial courts had no jurisdiction over those ancient services which were of the essence of the tenure. They were confined to the enforcement of those which had grown with the development of lordship along manorial lines. For the exaction of all rents and services the process of the court baron in England as a whole is by distress upon chattels at the order of the court and, in default, escheat *pro defectu servitii*. In Kent every manor has two clearly contrasted machines for enforcing service, the normal procedure of distress, and the process of *gavelate*. The rents of the inland and the recent additions to the rents of the outland are subject to distress. Inland tenements can be resumed by the lord on judgement of his court for default. The proprietary right of the gavelkinder, on the contrary, is much more sacred. If gavelkind service is withheld, the lord cannot distrain on the land. He must proclaim the deficiency in three successive sessions of his court, and after the third he may appear in the county and make his complaint in full court before the sheriff. Only so may a gavelkind tenement be declared waste, or gavelate, and the lord cannot enter upon it until it has lain waste for a year and a day. Finally, it is even then recoverable by the defaulter upon payment of a sum which is variously stated as nine years' rent or the wer-gild of the forfeited tenant. We have here not only a reminder of the special sanctity of folk-right in gavelkind, but a criterion of the services which that folk-right sanctioned. At Minster, says the survey, *qui non pacant gabulum suum et horsaver suum ad terminos constitutos solebant accusari de gavelate. De firma et de averherde et de avercorn et de dono vicecomitis et de agnis debet dominus distringere.*[1] The dues which have been added by the lord within traditional memory, the firma, the gift of lambs, and the labour commutation of average, being in their nature manorial, come under the seigneurial right of distress and escheat: gavelate covers only the gafol, and the average

[1] *B.B.* i. 60.

which has not been commuted. Thus for two services, and
for two only, the gavelkinders are withdrawn from the
custom and court of the manor of Minster and enjoy the
custom of Kent. From this a vital conclusion may be drawn.
Since gafol and average are the only services recoverable by
gavelate, they should be those of the Minster services
enjoined by gavelkind, those which, irrespective of later
accretions, may be exacted from gavelkind tenants at all
times and in all places, and are, presumably, its ancient and
authentic service. They are not of manorial custom, nor en-
forceable in the court of the manor, but national liabilities
arising from the tenure of all who hold by gavelkind, the
common law of the ancient kingdom, protected by the
county. The service of gavelkind, therefore, is presented to
us as peculiarly free and as an integral part of a common law
of Kent protected by the courts of the realm. When the
county declares its custom and secures its recognition by the
king's justices in eyre in the *Constitutiones Cancie—que le
comunaute de Kent cleiment auer en tenementz de gavylekende e
en gentz gavylekendes*—immunity from increase of service
stands, as part of a body of common custom, with freedom
of inheritance, the partible birthright of heirs, wardship and
dower, the conditions of escheat, and the gavelate protection
of the freehold. Matters of manorial custom in other parts
of England are here of common right. The mutual consis-
tency of the provisions, the sustained contrast with the rules
of ordinary villeinage or free tenure, and the recurrence of old
English terms and formulae point to a very early origin.
*Ces sont les usages de gavylekendes en Kent, que furent devaunt
le conquest, en le conquest, et totes houres jeskes en ca*, is their
conclusion, and, with the necessary reservations, we may
accept the Constitutions as the resumption of the series of
native Kentish codes.

I take it, then, that the service of gavelkind together with
its privileges of status, of wardship and dower, its ingrained
right of kindred, was not determined by the needs of the
manor, nor imposed in the right of the manor's lord. It was a
common obligation upon the folk of a kingdom, correlative
to a common folk-right. The whole complex of custom,
personal status, law of inheritance, co-operation for tillage,

service, seems, indeed, to stand aside from manorial commit-
ments, to antedate the manor, and to have been caught into
its machinery at a comparatively late epoch. It is a common
law which has passed out of the public forum in so far as the
courts of the folk have passed into private hands. In the
following section I shall endeavour to reconstruct its original
condition as a common folk-right, and the courts and administrations in which it had its course, and this must be the
justification of so much preoccupation with the small affairs
of the hamlet. The peasant custom of Kent is part of
English history because it bears marks of freedom, kindred-
right and antiquity, which carry it back to the common
stock of Germanic custom, and because it determined society
and government in the Kentish kingdom in the days of its
independent power.

(c) THE LATHE

The Kentish folk and their custom as we have seen them
appear in the thirteenth century as survivals from a vanished
age. The law of status and inheritance, though modernized
in its application in the king's courts, differed little from
Ripuarian and Salian custom of 500 years ago, as it ran in
the hamlets of the Kentish countryside. Private law has
come almost unchanged to the Middle Ages *a tempore a quo
non extat memoria*, has resisted the virus of feudalism, and
presents us with the essentials of English life as it was in the
days of the English settlement.

And if the England of the invasions has survived in the
lowest sphere in peasant custom, is it not reasonable to look for
its principles in the sphere of government? Is it not possible that successive Saxon and Norman conquests may have
failed to wrest justice or administration from their bed in
common life, and that the bailiffries and honours of Norman
Kent may preserve the frame of government of the days
when Kent was a kingdom? If so we shall recover its outlines in the relation of the peasant hamlets to the outer world,
in their suit and service to the larger units of which they
form a part.

As we strip away the superstructure of the Middle Ages
an older phase of British life rises into view. It is the phase

which succeeded the vaguely apprehended migratory period of Tacitus and the sagas. It has nothing provisional about it and it lasted for centuries in England, leaving its mark on all later history. The organization of certain British peoples in Wales, in Scotland, in Northumbria, was then provincial rather than manorial or feudal. There were as yet few great lords between the free man and the king, and the common free men were the main stock of the folk. Even then, rents and services were owed to the king, and for the reception of such dues provinces, shires, commotes, 'lay into' royal centres which were the seats of reeves. They were king's towns, *villae regales*. Such a society we cannot call feudal, yet we misrepresent it equally by calling it tribal, for tribal is a word which carries with it, rightly or wrongly, notions of a clannish, migratory life, divorced from the soil and from stable government. The tribe as a political notion has never extricated itself from the German forests, while there was nothing formless about these British and Anglian kingdoms. They were firmly rooted in the soil, lived under a strongly organized kingship, gave way to feudalism slowly.

Scir or commote are not reproduced in detail in Kent, where alodial property introduces a new factor from the first. It is not likely that the same elements in the same combination were ever found in any two racial settlements. But in broad outline Northumbria, Wales, and Kent agree. The Northumbrians called these large administrations *scirs*, and the Kentings had something like them and called them *lathes*. Some difficulty has always been felt about this word lathe; but, in fact, it is rare rather than obscure. Actually, *lathe* is the exact synonym of *soke*, and is used with precisely the same inflexions of meaning as the more familiar word. *Lathe* can mean *secta curiae*, as in the formula *infangthief*, oath and ordeal, *and preo motlaeðu ungeboden on xii monðum*;[1] it can mean 'jurisdiction' in the abstract, as when a Bromley charter is witnessed by all the lawful folk of west Kent where *ðæt land and ðæt læð to lið*;[2] or it can mean the land over which such jurisdiction extends,[3] either the whole

---

[1] *Cod. Dip.* DCCCXCVI. [2] Ibid. MCCLVIII.
[3] The schedule of the Rochester bridge-bot, 'Aeglesfortha and of eallan tham laethe the therto lith', Lambarde, *Perambulation*, p. 344.

province—in such normal phrases as the *Lathe of Sherwin-hope*—or of some smaller unit possessing immunity from the lathe.[1] Wherever a man of the Danelagh would say *soke*, a Kentishman would say *lathe*.

With all these parallels to draw upon it does not seem too bold to look for a 'provincial' phase in Kentish history, from which the gavelkind may have derived those quasi-public obligations and customs which it carried rather incongruously into the age of feudalism. It must be obvious that the peculiar independence of the gavelkind hamlets as we have seen them would strain the loose organization of a province less than the interlocking machinery of a manor. Their geographical isolation prevented regular labour upon a demesne, and their peasant freehold was strong to resist the demands of manorial lordship. It would be hard to get more from them than corn or money, loans of plough and plough-team, help in harvest, or carriage of crops and timber. Such dues could be exacted without trouble or friction from the scattered hamlets of the outland, and were not incompatible with the honour of the *francigena* in the heroic age. In Wales, in Northumbria, in Friesland, among the Icelandic settlers, such services were rendered to a prince or magnate by his people, with no thought that freedom was impaired. They were the natural resources of primitive royalty.

With this in our minds, we shall understand why the many variations of gavelkind service display a common basis beneath their variety. Though details may vary from manor to manor, it is provincial and not manorial custom.

Indeed, throughout the early northern world the tie between king and subject took forms strange to Norman eyes, for the hierarchy of shire, hundred, manor, was preceded by a simple order upon one plane, in which the king's vill gave justice in all causes, and took quasi-manorial renders from the community, while the fullest political and civil freedom was compatible with obligations which were considered servile in the age of Bracton. That gavelkind originated in some such provincial scheme is made almost certain by two facts, first, that only the gavelkind hamlets of the peasantry are hidated for public service while the

[1] Domesday Monachorum, f. 6 c: 'Sandwic . . . est laeth et hundret in se ipso.'

alod is not,[1] and, second, that these sulungs and yokes are unreal as regards the actual acreage of the tenements, and only find an explanation as fractions of a larger provincial assessment by lathes.

The geld assessment of Domesday in a long series of important manors covers neither more nor less than the outland tenures, the same units defending the manor against the king for geld, and themselves against the manor for the dues of peasant custom. In Thanet, *Monocstune T.R.E. pro xx solins se defendebat. Et modo pro xviij*,[2] while two centuries later *apud Moneketone sunt xviij swlingae de gavelkende*.[3] In Eastrey,[4] Ickham,[5] Minster in Thanet,[6] Wye,[7] Adisham,[8] and Southfleet,[9] the sulungs for gavelkind service to the manor of the thirteenth century are the sulungs for geld of Domesday. Even apparent discrepancies between the two assessments prove their original identity. Norborne, which defended itself for 30 sulungs T.R.W.,[10] has 22½ sulungs of gavelkind in the thirteenth-century roll of the *donum vice-comitis*,[11] but the 30 are completed by the tenements of knights and free-tenants. Turning to Domesday, we find these frank-fees in the tenures of Oidelard, Gislebertus, and others, *qui tenent de terra villanorum huius manerii* 7½ sulungs. Thus, it is clear that the 30 sulungs of Domesday are the *terra villanorum* of 1086 and the sulungs of gavelkind of 1300. The outland, the gavelkind, is the geldable of Domesday. The inland has no fiscal obligation: *dominium et pars monachorum nunquam geldaverunt vel consuetudines fecerunt. Sed milites et ceteri homines per omnia defendebant*.[12] It is not easy to exaggerate the importance of this fact. Clearly, since the hidation for geld coincides with the hidation for manorial service, there is one scheme for geld and manorial dues, and we must believe that of the two systems—the manors or the royal administration—one accepted a cadastral

[1] Cf. the case in the *Eyre of Kent*, ed. Bolland (Selden Society), iii. 193.
[2] D.B. i. 4 b.   [3] B.M. Add. MS. 6159, f. 28 a.   [4] D.B. i. 5 a.
[5] Ibid. i. 5 a.   [6] Ibid. i. 12 a.   [7] Ibid. i. 11 b.   [8] Ibid. i. 5 a.
[9] Ibid. i. 5 b.   [10] Ibid. i. 12 b.   [11] *B.B.* i. 77.
[12] P.R.O. Excheq. Augm. Off. M.B. 27, f. 13 b; cf. also the case of Mongeham: D.B. i. 12 b, and 'An Eleventh-Century Inquisition of St. Augustine's, Canterbury', ed. A. Ballard, in *The British Academy Records of Social and Economic History*, iii (1920), p. 22, with the editor's comment.

plan at second hand from the other. Either the manors were built up from the units of some royal circumscription, or the king seized upon the units of a pre-existing manorial system and laid his geld upon them. We are led, therefore, to question whether or no the scheme of sulungs antedated the manor as a social institution.

Fortunately, it is a simple matter to obtain an answer. If the sulungs arose purely out of the natural growth of the manorial estates, as a means of admeasuring the tenements and their liabilities, their total for the county, or for any area above the grade of the manor, will be irregular. Symmetrical planning will appear within the sphere of the private estate only and will be determined by it. If, on the other hand, the hidation was part of an older royal administration, we shall find a scheme based on larger and more regular units than the manors. In fact, the unreality of the sulungs and juga as regards the manors and the acres of the fields is so glaring as to need little proof. The sulungs of the manor of Chislet of St. Augustine are nominally of 200 fiscal acres each. Actually, the field acreage of the four of which we have record is 185, 200, 27, 75.[1] At Newchurch, with a nominal sulung of 160 acres, we get dolae or yokes of 40, 42, $46\frac{1}{2}$, $50\frac{1}{2}$, $22\frac{1}{2}$, and 60 real acres.[2] At Wye and Gillingham the disparity is wider still. There are juga of 120, $59\frac{3}{4}$, 37, 42 real acres at Wye;[3] at Gillingham of 23, $30\frac{3}{4}$, 39, $47\frac{1}{2}$, $132\frac{1}{4}$, 232.[4] Clearly the sulungs are useless as admeasuring the soil of the manor. They are unreal fiscal units, whose meaning must be found in some wider scheme of taxation. This is not peculiar to the south-east. In the north, too, and the west the carucation is not manorial.

The basis of the cadastre may vary. In some districts it seems to be national or sub-national, as in the rounded assessment of 500 carucates of north Lancashire. In some, as here, I believe, a smaller unit may be taken, the hundred of parts of Wessex, or the 600 carucate units of Yorkshire and Lincolnshire. In Kent, as the real inequality of the tenements warns us against looking for the meaning of their

[1] *B.B.* i. 105.　　　　　　　　　[2] B.M. Add. MS. 37018.
[3] P.R.O. Excheq. Augm. Off. M.B. 56.
[4] B.M. Add. MS. 33902.

assessment in manorial requirements, so their equality of unreal, fiscal acreage points towards the older institution of the lathe. Really unequal within their single manors, the sulungs are fiscally uniform from manor to manor within the lathe. The lathes of Eastrey[1] and Borowara[2] work upon a uniform sulung of 200 fiscal acres, that of Limenewara[3] on one of 160; Aylesford lathe[4] has a 180-acre sulung *de consuetudine regionis*; at Milton,[5] where the acreage of the sulung is not known, the Lacys describe their lands as assessed *sicut alie terre sullyngate in patria*. As they lie in our modern map these lathes do not promise the equality demanded of an equitable fiscal scheme. Their areas vary considerably, the 260,000 acres of Scray occupying the whole coastal plain from Chatham to Whitstable, about half the Weald and the upper valley of the Stour, while the 127,000 acres of Shipway contain only the Romney Level and the high land surrounding the Marsh. As we move backward in time, however, this excessive inequality gives way to smaller and more equal areas. St. Augustine's lathe divides into two, and Milton breaks away from Scray.[6]

Domesday reveals a regular arrangement in groups of 160 or 80 sulungs, each group forming a solid block of adjacent hundreds, and one, two, or more such groups exactly occupying the area of each lathe according to the hidage of 1066. Beginning from the west, the Borowara Lest of Domesday contains a group of approximately 160 sulungs, the Isle of Thanet,[7] separated from the mainland by the river Wansum, and the lower Stour valley, with its centre at Canterbury, the *borough* from which the *borowara* took their name. To the south and west of Borowara lathe lies Limouara lathe, the district once subject to the ancient royal curtis of Lyminge, sometimes known as the *regio merscwariorum*, or province of the marshmen. It contains a single

[1] Library of the Dean and Chapter of Canterbury, Reg. C, f. 16 b; ibid., Reg. J, f. 35 a.   [2] *B.B.* i. 95, 197.
[3] D.B. i. 2 a; B.M. Add. MS. 37018, ff. 44 et seq.
[4] *Registrum Roffense*, p. 65.   [5] *B.B.* i. 283.
[6] B.M. MS. Arundel 310, f. 111 a.
[7] Thanet has many features which would make its existence as a separate unit plausible, and a wrong identification of Estursete Hd. as Westgate in Thanet led me to allot it 80 sulungs. (*Eng. Hist. Rev.* xliv (1929), 613, 614.) It must, however, on the ground of hidage be merged with the Borowara.

unit of $80\frac{9}{32}$ sulungs. The modern lathe of Scray includes
three such units of 80. Of these, Milton, consisting of a
single large manor, is itself a half-lathe in Domesday and de-
fends itself for 80 sulungs. It maintained its administrative
independence until the sixteenth century, when it became
merged in the neighbouring lathe of Scray or Sherwinhope.
The *villa regis* of Faversham may have had slightly more than
80 sulungs, or perhaps have been rounded off to 100 by
the addition of Reculver and Whitstable. Wye makes up
the rest of Scray lathe and has about it $80\frac{11}{48}$ sulungs. The
modern lathe of Aylesford contains three sub-divisions; of
these Hoo Hundred, $61\frac{3}{4}$, Rovecestre, $4\frac{1}{2}$, Ceteham, $12\frac{1}{2}$,
made up $78\frac{1}{2}$ sulungs; Aihorde with Medestane is $79\frac{3}{4}$
sulungs, and the rest of the lathe is occupied by a double
unit of $159\frac{1}{2}$ sulungs.

In the most westerly lathe of the county, Sutton-at-Hone,
we have the group of Achestan, $49\frac{3}{4}$, Helmestrei, $26\frac{3}{4}$, Oistre-
ham, 4, making $80\frac{1}{2}$ sulungs as a whole. The rest of the lathe
is irregular, consisting of $35\frac{1}{2}$ sulungs in the border hundreds
of Bronlei, Grenviz, and Litelai. It is possible that they
have at some time lost land to the Surrey hundreds of
Waleton or Brixistan, and that it is for this reason that Sutton
is known as *Dimidius Lest de Suttone* in the Domesday
survey. The lathe of Eastrey also presents difficulties. In
all probability its four hundreds arose from the division of
two earlier groups, Beusberg-Cornilai and Wingham-
Eastrey. Though Beusberg and Cornilai together make up
$79\frac{5}{8}$ sulungs, and Wingham has a round 40 sulungs, Eastrey
has $54\frac{1}{8}$, so that the total of the second group is abnormal.
Folkestone is a half-unit of 40 sulungs imbedded in the lathe
of Eastrey, but reckoned in the lathe of Shipway for geld.
The two hundreds of Whitstaple, $1\frac{3}{4}$, and Reculver, $24\frac{1}{4}$, are
in the north of the Domesday lathe of the Borowara. There
has evidently been a slight change in the lathe boundaries
in this area, but the hidation is correctly recorded, for the
whole mass of the lathes of Eastrey and Borowara, together
with the extravagants, Whitstaple, Reculver, and Folkestone,
make up 320, or, to be exact, 319 sulungs, or 4 units of 80.
Nothing has been lost, but the original line of division is
slightly blurred.

The plan of the county is one of 11 units which approach within a sulung of the round 80 or 160. The lathes grow smaller as we go backward in time, and as we pass the Conquest the process is accelerated. We hear nothing of the large lathes of Sutton or Scray, much of the smaller units. Already in a document which can hardly be later than Domesday, the English schedule of the Rochester bridge-work, the 80 sulungs of Maidstone-Eyhorn are spoken of as *Hollingaburna and ealla that lathe*,[1] and though, to my knowledge, the vernacular term appears only once in pre-Conquest charters,[2] the lathe must be the *regio* of the grants of the eighth century, where such forms as *Limenweara*—the *Limowart* of Domesday—alternate with bilingual phrases such as *in regione on Liminum*.

Of these *regiones* the charters have preserved the names of six, Eastrey,[3] Lyminge,[4] Faversham,[5] Hoo,[6] Rochester,[7] and Rainham,[8] the first two being the Domesday lathes, the next three 80-sulung units in Domesday, and the sixth in all probability the ancient centre of the 80 sulungs of Milton. Wye is not spoken of as a *regio*, but it appears as a substantial area by the name Wywara as early as the eighth century.[9] Thus, in the earlier charters the unit of assessment of the Domesday hidage gains in reality at the expense of the large composite lathes of 1066.

The service of the gavelkinder, therefore, is not proportionate to his holding in the manor, and is proportionate to his assessment to the lathe. To what purpose, then, were the lathes first carved into sulungs and yokes? Not for the manor: not for the Danegeld, either, for they are older than the Danegeld, older than the supremacy of Wessex. Rather, to assess the countryside for precisely the same gafol and

[1] Lambarde, *Perambulation of Kent*, p. 344.

[2] *Cod. Dip.* MCCLVIII.

[3] *Cart. Sax.* 254: 'In regione Eastrgena ubi nominatur Duningcland.' Ibid. 332.

[4] Ibid. 341: 'In regione on Liminum et in loco ubi . . . Kasing Burnan appellatur.'

[5] Ibid. 341: 'In partibus suburbanis regis oppidulo Fefresham'; ibid. 353: 'In regione qui dicitur Febres ham.'

[6] Ibid. 159: 'In regione quae vocatur Hohg in loco qui dicitur Andscohesham.'

[7] Ibid. 199: 'In regione Caestruuara.'

[8] Ibid. 335: 'In regione suburbanaque regis oppido ibi ab incolis Roeginga hám nuncupato.'

[9] Ibid. 141: 'On Weowera wealde'.

service which we find it paying in the Middle Ages to the private lord and the manor, but to assess it for the king. The gafol and precariae once went to maintain the Crown, and were the king's feorm as the king enjoyed it in so many Teutonic provinces of the pre-feudal age. The feorm was exacted by the king's reeve, accounted for in the curia of the *villa regis*, determined by reckoning the lathe at 80 reputed ploughlands and laying on each an equal obligation.

The groups of 80 sulungs which compose the Domesday lathes are proved by the earliest charters to lie in a special relation to the ancient centres of royal power. The regio is called as a rule after a *villa regis*, some *regia et famosa villa* where moots were held and the king from time to time held his court. The lathe of the Limenewara takes its name from the *cortis quae appellatur Liminge*,[1] *mea regia villa*;[2] that of the Wywara is named from the *villa regalis . . . quae nominatur Wyth*,[3] *illa famosa villa qui dicitur Vueae*.[4] Aylesford is a centre of justice.[5] The lathe of the Borowara is clearly named from the *burh* of Canterbury, that of the Caestruuara[6] or Cæstersæta[7] from the *chester* of Rochester. The regiones were the provinces of reeves. One Aethelnoth, who made his will between 805 and 831, is recorded as *gerefa to Eastorege*.[8] In 747 the *procurator* Uualhhun is found controlling the weald pastures of the Caestruuara.[9] A Canterbury charter of 805 speaks of Aldhun *qui in hac regali villa in huus civitatis praefectus fuit*.[10] Three *praefecti*, whose provinces are not specified, witness a charter of 696,[11] their crosses appearing before the common laity, and three *praepositi* appear in 804,[12] amid a galaxy of bishops, duces, and comites. Evidently these were men of importance. There is every sign of such a system of royal prefects as would accompany the government of the lathes from a series of provincial capitals.[13]

The outland sulungs of the manors, therefore, are also units of roundly assessed lathes, which themselves serve

1 Ibid. 73.   2 Ibid. 419.   3 Ibid. 191.   4 Ibid. 449.
5 Ibid. 1064.   6 Ibid. 175, 199.   7 Ibid. 303.
8 Ibid. 318.   9 Ibid. 175.   10 Ibid. 319.   11 Ibid. 91.
12 Ibid. 316, 319, 321.
13 Cf. Mr. H. M. Chadwick's remarks on this subject, *Studies on Anglo-Saxon Institutions*, pp. 250 et seq.

capital townships and are subject to provincial reeves. The
lathes are very substantial entities. The grouping of all the
agricultural population under the *villae regales* overrides
all other landmarks. Graveney is not in the hundred of
Faversham, but, since it is in the regio, the lathe, it is *in
regione suburbana ad oppidum regis.*[1] Higham is not in
Rochester Hundred, but it is in the regio of the Caestruuara.[2]
The hundred, which the nomenclature of the charters
ignores, and which is mentioned in no Kentish charter before
the Conquest, seems a modern and transient thing in comparison with the lathe.

The unity which this proves was economic as well as
social and governmental. The lathe presented itself to the
official mind of the eighth century primarily as an area
'suburban' to, or in the vernacular, 'lying in to', such royal
towns as Lyminge, Faversham, or Wye. Even in the Middle
Ages these are more than the meeting places of courts. Each
of the twelve or thirteen king's tuns acted as *caput* of all the
royal land which lay within the boundary of its lathe, and
the distribution of this land gives a diagrammatic proof
that the lathe was an economic whole. Blocks of arable,
marsh, or wood, distributed near and far throughout the
lathe, show that its boundary is also the containing line of a
scattered royal estate.

The interpenetration of the lathe by the inland of the
royal vill is particularly clear at Milton. The Court of
Ancient Demesne of the manor of Milton claims jurisdiction
over eighteen parishes of the mainland and the whole of
Sheppey, except for the Isle of Harty—its jurisdiction,
therefore, is coincident with the lathe of Milton.[3] In 1575
the Queen held land in demesne as of her manor of Milton
in the nine parishes of Halstow, Newington, Minster-in-
Sheppey, Milton, Bredgar, Stockbury, Tunstall, Bapchild,
and Sittingbourne, some of it being in the extreme outward
parts of the lathe. By the time of Domesday the regio of
Faversham had dwindled from 80 sulungs to become a
manor of no more than $7\frac{1}{2}$ sulungs,[4] but this so-called
manerium was much more than the nucleus of land in the

---

[1] *Cart. Sax.* 341.   [2] Ibid. 199.
[3] Hasted, History of Kent, ii. 624.   [4] D.B. i. 2 b.

parish of Faversham. In the second year of Henry II the amount allowed to the sheriff for the *terrae datae* of Faversham was £100,[1] half the value of the lathe in 1066.[2] To the king's demesne in the two parishes of Faversham Within and Without we must add the land at Ospringe, now a separate royal honour, but included with Faversham in 1086. At the Dissolution there were still demesne lands in Boughton Hundred, in the parishes of Hernhill, Dunkirk, Graveney, and Boughton, and in Faversham Hundred at Preston, the two Favershams, Goodnestone, and the whole Isle of Harty with its barton of Abbot's Court.[3] In addition, we must reckon with the original demesne the knights' fees, sixteen in all, of the abbot's *servitium debitum*. These were not in existence ten years after the foundation of the abbey in 1166, and were created, according to the normal Kentish custom, from the frank fee or inland. The knights' fees lay in the parishes of Baddlesmere, Buckland, Throwley, Preston, Eastling, Luddenham, Ospringe, Norton, and Newnham.[4] The original inland of Faversham, then, seems to have been distributed over almost every parish of the lathe and over the two principal hundreds into which it was divided. Other lathes have suffered more from subinfeudation and division than these, but where substantial fragments of lathes have been conveyed to the churches, we find the same tendency for the inland to lie in every quarter of the lathe. Folkestone, the capital of a half-lathe of 40 sulungs, has demesne in five parishes, Folkestone, Alkham, Hougham, Newington, and Hawking.[5] Minster, which is paramount over three-quarters of the ancient administration of Thanet, has demesne scattered about the Island at Salmstone, Newland, Alland, Calis, and the barton of Hengrave.[6] Thus, the demesne of the lathe forms an organic whole, a single estate administered from the *villa regis* and penetrating the whole lathe in a network of royal alod.

The king's pasture of the *villae regales* is also planned to the scale of the lathe. In the allotment of the king's

[1] Pipe Roll, 2 Henry II.   [2] D.B., *passim.*
[3] Dugdale, *Monasticon*, iv. 579.   [4] Ibid. iv. 569.
[5] P.R.O. *Inq. p.m.* C. Hen. III, File 29 (1), and 40 (7).
[6] Thorne in *Decem Scriptores*, 2202.

woodland there is a symmetry between lathe and lathe which suggests design, and design of which the lathe is the determining unit. To each *villa regis* there are appertinent one or more areas of several forest, the king's firth or *snade*,[1] either lying within the hidated area, or upon the edge of the Weald adjacent to the area set aside for the men of the lathe. Most commonly the former is hill-pasture, *cyninges dun*, or *mons regis*,[2] and to this some half-dozen Kingsdowns or Kingstons owe their place on the map to-day. These royal woods have left their mark in early charters, for every king's town had a several wood within its lathe jurisdiction. Faversham had two such woods, Faversham Blean, in Blean Forest, where the Abbot still had 1,100 acres at the Dissolution,[3] and the king's snade of Faversham, 12 miles off, in the Weald—the modern Kingsnorth Wood in Ulcombe.[4] Canterbury, also, had its share of Blean Forest astride the boundary of the lathes of the Borowara and Faversham, possessing the eastern half with its outlyer of Buckholt,[5] and it had, too, the long-vanished wood of Harethum,[6] perhaps in Kingstone by Barham. Charters from Cesterwara[7] and Aylesford lathes constantly refer to pasture *in monte regis*,[8] in the 'King's Down' or *snade*. The woods of the former

[1] *Cart. Sax.* 442: 'Unus singularis silva . . . quem nos theodoice snad nominamus.' Ibid. 343, 7 ðet firhde bituihn longanleah 7 ðem suðtune 7 ða snadas illuc pertinentia. Ibid. 459.

[2] Ibid. 418: 'et in monte regis quinquaginta carrabas lingnorum.'

[3] Hasted, ii. 707; Southouse, *Monasticon Favershamense*, p. 55.

[4] *Cart. Sax.* 459 (A.D. 850). This charter places the south border of Lenham as being the 'cyningessnade to Feferesham'. This is the modern wood of Kingsnorth, which form is the usual development of 'king's snade' in the later Middle Ages. The Abbot of Faversham still held Kyngsnorth, then a manor, in Henry VIII's reign; *Monasticon*, iv. 578.

[5] *Cart. Sax.* 869: Wickhambreux granted with 'þæt den on Blean Earneshyrst'; *Pat. Rolls*, 1229: 'Communa pasture in Ble'que pertinet in Herbaldown'; *Cart. Sax.* 248: Land in Ickham 'mid thaem denbaerum . . . in boc holte and in blean'.

[6] Ibid. 248 (A.D. 791). 'In hara thum c fothra wido and twegra wegna gang wintres sumeres.' The locality of Harethum is given by the metes of 7 sulungs in Barham (ibid. 328). This would be consonant with Harethum being on the site of the modern Kingstone—possibly itself a corruption of 'Kingsdown'.

[7] Ibid. 486: A haga and 10 acres in Rochester 'et x carros cum silvo honestos in monte regis'.

[8] Ibid. 418: Land at Snodland and Holborough . . . 'et in monte regis quinquaginta carrabas lingnorum'; *Cod. Dip.* DCLXXXVIII. Six sulungs at Wouldham and 'cxx swina ingang æt Horshyrste on ðæm snade'. *Cart. Sax.* 263 (A.D. 791): Pastus unius gregis juxta theningden et L porcorum binnan snæde.'

must have been Kingsdown by Rochester, and Kingsnorth in Hoo, while Aylesford in the tenth century had its Kingswood on the northern border of the parish and extending into East Malling.[1] For all these there is early charter evidence. To turn to more doubtful cases, charters convey wood-rights in the king's wood of the Lymenewara,[2] though I do not know its site. There is no record evidence for Milton, Eastry, or the 80-sulung group at Axton, but each preserves its Kings Down to-day, Milton and Axton in the parishes of those names, and Eastry in Kingsdown in Ringwold. The several wood of Wye does not appear before the Conquest, but its Kingswood, in a detached part of Wye parish, and its king's snade—Kingsnorth parish—retained their connexion with the manor of Wye throughout the Middle Ages.

For two reasons these several royal woods show that the *villa regis* was regarded as the caput of the whole lathe for the royal demesne. The dependence of the king's wood on the king's vill transcends the boundaries of townships and hundreds. The *silva regis* is not often in the township of its capital vill, seldom in the same hundred. Faversham Blean is not in the parish or hundred of Faversham, but in the hundred of Boughton. The king's snade of Wye is in the hundred of Blackborne. Harethum was not within the bounds of Canterbury, but in the hundred of Barham. The king's down of Milton was on the extreme eastern boundary of the lathe some 5 miles from the border of the capital vill. The general impression given by the charters is that a line of king's firths and snades ran along the northern edge of the Weald where they would be most conveniently placed and nearest to the king's towns. It was clearly sufficient that the *silva regis* should be within the lathe or the weald of the lathe; parish and hundred counted for nothing. Again, although the men of the lathe had no such general right of use as they had in the Weald, the king was generous enough in his grants of timber and pasture to enable us to trace the

[1] *Cal. Inq. p.m.* v. 116. 'In the King's wood by Malling'; *Cart. Sax.* 779 (A.D. 942–6); *Calendar of Charter Rolls*, i. 293: Malling Wood a member of the manor of Aylesford.

[2] *Cart. Sax.* 507: Eight sulungs at Mersham . . . 'et iiij carris transductionem in silba regis . . . hubi alteri homines silbam cedunt, hoc est in regis communione'.

outline of the system, and the wood-rights of each capital were confined to the lathe in which it stood. Use in the king's woods was granted only to tenants whose lands lay within the lathe, and to these it was granted for tenures far and near, without respect to the distance at which they lay from the administrative centre. Thus the *silva regis* of the royal estates shows the unity of the lathe. Its size, its remoteness from the *villa regis*, its lack of relation to the subordinate organizations of township and hundred, the freedom with which a right of use is granted to all the manors of the lathe, all suggest that it once subserved some larger purpose than that of demesne wood to the diminished royal manors of the Middle Ages. Like the inland, it seems to have been built to some wider economic plan than is displayed by the rigid manorial divisions of Domesday. In fact, the king's estates were identified, not with the manor, but with the lathe. Wide apart as they may lie, in different townships, in different hundreds, the isolated fields of the *terra regis* are part of a single property, are supervised by one reeve, their profits appear upon one roll of account, they are tilled jointly by such manual services as arise from the outland. One boundary, and one only, of the many that conflict together, borghus, civil and ecclesiastical township, or hundred, suffices to circumscribe them—the lathe boundary. One centre alone receives their profits and controls their exploitation, the *villa regis* which is the lathe's capital. The *terra regis* was organized by lathes, and to this degree the lathe was a unified area with a single economic framework, devised as a symmetrical part of a national whole, and going back to a period of antiquity beyond which we cannot reach.

It is impossible to believe that this was the lathe's sole or principal function. The king's inland, though widely distributed, was smaller in extent than the outland, and the outland determined the size and the form of the lathes. They were circumscriptions of 80 sulungs, and the sulung was not a measure of demesne but of outland. The aspect in which the lathe is most directly presented to us is as a unit of the general settlement, of that community of free ceorls holding their land by the Custom of Kent which is pre-eminently the folk of the Kentings.

Thus we shall understand the nature of the lathe most
fully if we can determine its authority over the sulungs.
What is the relation of the individual sulungs in gavelkind
to those groups of 80 which have already taken form by the
beginning of the eighth century, in the days when the
Kentish kingdom still preserved its integrity? The law of
the Middle Ages is clear in its answer. The lathe, as at
Milton, is a manor, the gavelkinders are tenants, the sulungs
are tenements of the manor.[1] Because the king was the
greatest landowner in the lathe of Milton, because his court
of Milton did justice upon its men and received their service,
the Norman surveyors spoke of the *manerium de Middeltune*.
But this is to make of Milton an economic unity fuller and
more sharply realized than the Dark Ages knew, to make the
king a feudal lord and his power over the gavelkind dominical, and to do this is to ignore the most fundamental characteristic of Jutish tenure, the isolation and self-sufficiency of
the alod and its impotence to create a dominium over the
gavelland *ex propria vi*. To bring together the whole ground
of the lathe under the real ownership of the king would be
to ignore the inherent freedom of the gavelkinders, and to
give an unreal simplicity to the origin of the lathe.

Nevertheless, the medieval judgement upon the status of
the gavelland is not to be ignored. The fact that the sulungs
in gavelkind could come to be regarded as tenements of a
manor, of which the lathe was the frame and the *villa regis*
the curia, certainly proves a long tradition of solidarity, and
there is much positive evidence to show that this tradition
was well founded. The men of the lathe were not a manorial
community, but we must think of the lathe as an economic
and social whole, and find its origin in the primitive grouping
of the Kentish people for justice, administration, and even
in a measure for agriculture.

It will perhaps be thought that the antiquity of the lathe
and its reality in the economy of the folk will be most surely
established if it be proved that all its hamlets co-operated for
one of the major processes of agriculture, since, while the

[1] P.R.O. Court Rolls, Portf. 181. 74: 'Tenementum quod fuit Willelmi Tebburd
in Scapeya' (in Milton); *Inq. p.m.* vii. 131: Swanton held of the manor of Milton in
gavelkind.

outlines of government and judicature may alter, change in the course of husbandry is hardly to be reckoned by centuries. In what sense, then, is it possible to regard the lathe as the constituent unit of the social and economic life of the folk, of that community which the Saxons lodged in the village? The principle of equality of birthright among heirs made constantly for division, and the one force counteracting it was the practice of joint cultivation by the family, in so far as that prevailed. In one sense, therefore, the unit of economic life could never be larger than the sulung-hamlet, and was even smaller than that of the Midlands, where village cultivation was the rule. This is true, not only of the arable lands, but of the pasture. It, too, was appropriated to individuals, and came under the rules of partible inheritance, so that, with few exceptions, there was no waste in the Kentish manor, but small enclosures, tuns, hammes, and teaghs. In the opinion of the courts there was no common land in Kent. One class of land, and that for a time only, defeated the Kentish genius for individual property. The great waste of the Weald, a hundred miles in length and a score in depth, defied delimitation, and, though each century carried encroachment and appropriation farther, Andred was still almost intact in 1086. During the Dark Ages it imposed upon the Jutes their one great experiment in intercommoning. For the intractable wild they were forced to find some unit larger than the individual or the family. This unit they found in the lathe.

At the earliest date, the eighth century, at which charters are available as evidence, the woodland of Kent is already divided into two classes, the *silva communis* or Weald proper, and the *silva regis*, according as it was reserved to the principal demesnes of the king or open to the common use of the countryside, and these royal and common woods were divided among the lathes and their *villae regales*. Each king's-town had its several *king's-wood*, *-firth*, *-snade*, or *-down*, and each lathe had a district allotted to it in the Weald within which the men of the lathe commoned together. There were thus in law something like a dozen *wealds*, though geographically the forest of Andred stretched unbroken from Romney Marsh to the border of Hampshire.

As early as 724 we meet with the Limenweara wealde and
the Weowara wealde, the wealds of Lyminge and Wye
lathes.[1] The former appears again in 786, together with
Burh waro waldo, the weald of the Burhwara.[2] In 747 we
find the reeve Uualhhun in dispute with the Bishop of
Rochester *circa porcorum pascua in silba quae appellatus est
Caestruuarouualth*.[3] In 801 land is granted at Bromey near
Rochester *adjectis iiij denberis in commune saltu id est on
Caestersaeta walda*.[4] The reference in both these charters is
clearly to a weald of the Chesterwara. We have, therefore,
contemporary evidence that separate common wealds were
attached to four of our 80-sulung lathes before the end of
the eighth century.

In the earliest charters these wealds are clearly commons.
The soil of Andred was no-man's-land; the right of pasture
was open to all men within the forest of the lathe in which
their arable tenements lay, and that right was one of use only.
Until the second decade of the ninth century the denes are
in publicis locis, in commune saltu.[5] It is in the common interest
only that pasture is limited,[6] and the use of the forest is
dictated by folk custom and controlled by the king and his
provincial reeves. So Cuthred promises *hanc prenominatam
terram tradere curabo ut communem silbam secundum antiquam
consuetudinem cum ceteris hominibus abeat*.[7] But with the
eighth century the phase of common use passes. As the
pressure on the Weald increases disputes arise, the king's
authority is brought to bear, and use hardens to prescription
under royal charter. In 747 the reeve Uualhhun *contra
episcopum Hrofensis ecclesiae sine intermissione congressum dis-
crimini fecit circa porcorum pascua in silba quae appellatus est
Caestruuarouualth*,[8] and the king for that reason concedes to

---

[1] *Cart. Sax.* 141: 'Haec sunt pascua porcorum . . . on Limen, Wearawalde (sci.
Limenwearawalde) . . . on Weowera wealde.'

[2] Ibid. 248: 'Mid 'thaem denbaerum in limen wero wealdo et in burh waro
uualdo.'   [3] Ibid. 175.   [4] Ibid. 303.

[5] Ibid. 260: 'Adjectis denberis in commune saltu, Bixle, Speldhirst, Meredaen
ðaer be eastan, and Rusteuuellae, and Teppanhyse.'

[6] Ibid. 191 (A.D. 762): 'unius gregis porcorum pascuam . . . in saltu Andoredo'.
Cod. Dip. CCXLI: 'Duobusque carris dabo licentiam silfam . . . secundum antiquam
consuetudinem . . . in commune silfa quam nos saxonicae in gemennisse dicimus'
(A.D. 839).

[7] *Cart. Sax.* 322 (A.D. 805).   [8] Ibid. 175.

St. Andrew *xij greguum porcorum ad serbandum in publicis locis, id est ut incoli nominandi dicunt Holanspic alius Paetlanhrygc, tercius Lindhrygc.* Custom is here in transition from common use to property in fixed localities. The reeve of the Chesterwara is losing control of the common weald of his lathe before the inroads of manorial property. The folk is losing its general right. But still the Weald was distinct from the cultivated land of the settlement and exempt from royal hidation.[1] At the time when the 80 sulungs of the lathes were carved out, the whole forest must have been a waste, and no man's fee was recognized there. The total of the hidated area of Andred in Domesday is 3⅝ sulungs.

Our charters, however, contain only echoes of the common use of the Weald in its primitive form. By the ninth century, it is usual to allot certain denes or pastures[2] to which the grantee is confined, and they begin to be spoken of as appertinent to his estate, *ðanne belimpoð ðer to ðam londe fif den . . . Broccesham ðes dennes nama, ðes oðres dennes nama Sænget hryg, Billan ora is ðes ðriddan nama, ðanne tpa denn an Gleppan felda.*[3] The *dene* is now a permanent appropriation of woodland within the *weald* of the *lathe* in which the main estate lies.

It is with the coming of seigneurial right in the Weald that the charters begin to record the denes by name, and so display the whole relation of lathe and forest before our eyes. The form of Kentish charters must be familiar, the grant, with its specification of the *terrae aratri*, the tracing of the metes of the hidated land, and then, often in invaluable contemporary idiom, identical in substance for the four counties of Kent, Surrey, Hampshire, and Sussex, the record by name, and often with some illuminating hint of custom, of the forest walks which custom or privilege annexes to the distant manor of the grant. In 966 Eadgar gave the 10 sulungs of Bromley to the Bishop of Rochester.[4] Together with the *terrae aratri*, and following their metes in the charter, *hæc utilitas silvarum ad eandem terram pertinet in Andrede: Billan-*

---

[1] In the Middle Ages sulungs and juga appear in the Weald for manorial purposes, but they are not geldable or subject to the ancient gafol.

[2] *Cart. Sax.* 496: 'Pascua porcorum quot nostra lingua denbera nominamus.'

[3] Ibid. 506.   [4] *Cod. Dip.* DXVIII.

oran be Lyndhyrste and on Glæppan felda, Scearndæn and par rihte wið Porndæn and Broccesham be eastan ea and tannera hole and trindhyrst. Of these walks, which were the forinsec pastures of Bromley in the tenth century, we can identify four on the ordnance map of to-day, Shernden, Lynhurst, and Broxham, in Edenbridge parish, Tannera hole as Tapner's Hole in the Park of Penshurst. The record of a single manor tells us little—that Bromley had a forest member lying 15 miles from its court—but a number of records, and especially an accumulation of records of manors from a single lathe will tell us much. With the 20-inch survey and a sufficiency of medieval surveys and pre-Conquest charters, we should be able to reconstitute the whole system of the lathe forests.

Fortunately we have ample record for doing so in outline. Charters are numerous and the names of the denes and their distribution change little. An almost contemporary charter of Ickham dated 785 gives the denes as Dun ualing daenn, Sandhyrst, Suið helming daenn.[1] At the end of Edward I's reign Swithelminden and Sandherste are still the two principal weald pastures of Ickham.[2] A charter of Lenham of 850[3] already mentions the denes of Thornden, Maplehurst, Friezley, and Frittingden, and these were the Lenham denes when the *Black Book* of St. Augustine's was compiled.[4] Even at the Conquest no great displacement occurred, and the only change of moment was the alienation of much of the weald of Sutton lathe to form Richard fitz Gilbert's Lowy of Tonbridge.

The simplest instance of all is that of Milton. In the thirteenth century the weald of this lathe was still preserved as a separate jurisdiction in Andred.[5] An inquisition of 1575[6] tells us that Milton held 42 denes in the hundred of Marden, and an entry in the *Rotuli Hundredorum* records *quod hundredum de Mardenn est membrum hundredi de Middiltun.*[7] We can therefore identify the weald of Milton as the

---

[1] *Cart. Sax.* 247.
[2] B.M. Add. MS. 6159, f. 33 b; Bodleian, Kentish Rolls, no. 12.
[3] *Cart. Sax.* 459.   [4] *B.B.* i. 250.
[5] *Pat. Rolls*, 1217: 'Sciatis quod concessimus Willelmo de Casinghm . . . dennos qui pertinent ad manerium nostrum de Middelton.'
[6] Hasted. iii. 28.   [7] *Rot. Hundr.* i. 201.

modern parish of Marden with the east part of Goudhurst
and the north of Staplehurst. Almost as simple is the
identification of the weald of the Lymenewara. Most of the
pasture of this lathe came to the great manor of Aldington,
the centre of the Archbishop's lands in Shipway. The weald
of Lymenewara is therefore delimited by the area in which
that manor is paramount—firstly, the hundred of Selbrih-
tenden, Sandhurst and Newenden parishes, the south
of Benenden and Rolvenden; secondly, most of Oxney
Hundred, in Wittersham, Stone, and Ebony; thirdly, the
south-eastern portion of Blackburn Hundred in Woodchurch and Kenardington, Halden; and lastly, a few denes
in Tenterden. Within this area, though Aldington has the
lion's share, other manors of Limenewara also have detached
members. Horton has denes in Shadoxhurst, Kenardington
and Acrise in Sandhurst, Snaves in Stone and Ebony. Thus,
the weald of the Lymenewara forms an irregular but compact
mass of two whole hundreds and parts of two others.

For the weald of Wye we have record of the denes of the
manors of Wye,[1] Kennington,[2] Mersham,[3] Brook,[4] Chartham,[5] Westwell,[6] Great[7] and Little Chart.[8] It is a somewhat
larger area to the north and west of the Lymenewara weald.
Apart from a few outlying members, it lies in the parishes of
Woodchurch, Hawkhurst, Cranbrook, Biddenden, Halden,
Smarden, Pluckley, and Bethersden, and forms a ribbon of
land some 4 miles by 8, running south-west from the
southern border of the lathe to the boundary of Sussex at
Hawkhurst. The weald of Faversham is already placed for
us in the ninth century when the *cyngessnade to Fefresham* lies
in Ulcombe;[9] the denes of Faversham lathe, appertinent to
the manors of Faversham,[10] Ospringe, Teynham, Eastling,
and Throwley, are gathered into a compact forest area
beside it, in Headcorn and the northern portions of Frittenden and Staplehurst. Thus, the weald of Faversham may be
traced back to the year 850.

[1] P.R.O. Excheq. Augm. Off. M.B. 18 and 56, *passim*.
[2] *B.B.* i. 235.
[3] *Cart. Sax.* 507; Library of the Dean and Chapter of Canterbury, Reg. J, f. 60 a.
[4] Ibid., f. 56 b.   [5] Ibid., f. 49 b.   [6] Ibid., f. 65 a.
[7] Ibid., f. 66 b.   [8] Ibid., f. 68 b.   [9] *Cart. Sax.* 459.
[10] *Monasticon Favershamense*, p. 55.

Moving west, we next come to the weald of the lathe of
Hollingborne, judicially merged in that of Aylesford, but
preserving its geographical homogeneity between the wealds
of Milton, Wye, and Faversham. Its centre is the parish of
Staplehurst, but it extends southward into Goudhurst, east-
ward into Frittenden and Cranbrook, and north-west into
Marden and Linton. Like Faversham weald, it can be carried
back to pre-Conquest times by the evidence of charters.
Aylesford lathe has its pasture in the eastern half of the
Lowy of Tonbridge, on either bank of the Medway in
Somerden, Speldhirst, and Brenchley.[1] Sutton lathe and the
manors of the extreme north-west shared the border parishes
of Chiddingstone, Hever, Cowden, and Edenbridge.[2] Lastly,
leaving its trace upon our map to-day, is the Weald of
Thanet, Tenet wara denne,[3] Tenwardenne,[4] Tenterden.

In so far as the term primitive is ever valid it is so of this
use of Andred. The mention of the Lymenewara and their
weald as early as 726 vouches for the Kentish lathe two
centuries before any other circumscription of government of
any of the English peoples. The plan of settlement, the
lathe of free folk with their common forest, is like the *Gau*
and its *Vogtholz* among the hamlet dwellers of north-western
Germany. They are institutions which this branch of the
Teutonic peoples shared in common in the last century of
the migrations. We have forced our way back in time to a
period when the Jutes have more in common with the
Franks of the Rhine than with their Saxon neighbours and
conquerors in Britain.

To turn, however, to other aspects of the lathe. It will not
have taken substance for us until we have shown that it was
not only the unit of the royal demesne and of the common
right in the Weald, but also the primary unit of the folk and
of the king's administration. We shall not expect it to play
that overmastering part in the life of the gavelkinders that the
village plays in the Midlands. The grain of Kentish society
is against the close and exacting association of the midland

[1] D.B. i. 3 a.
[2] B.M. MS. Cott. Julius, DII, f. 93 a: Plumstead has wood in Plumware-parroc,
Plummer's Parrock in Hever Parish.
[3] *Cart. Sax.* 1212: 'Tenet þara brocas.'
[4] Library of the Dean and Chapter of Canterbury, Reg. F., f. 43 a.

ploughing community. The part of the lathe in cultivation,
though real, is subsidiary, confined to the maintenance and
agistment of the common weald. But, setting cultivation
aside, the lathe has a vital place in custom. In the Midlands
the village-manor is a single organism, a community at once
in cultivation, in social life, and in servitude. In Kent the
hamlet has forestalled the growth of larger groups for
agriculture, but there is much that it cannot do. The Midland manor is the centre to which all the outward relations
of the villein are focused. It determines his status, his
rights, his obligations. Its court enforces them. It is the
framework in which his social life and much of his rudimen-
tary political life are lived. It sets and maintains him in his
customary relation to the outer world of feudalism. Gavelkind needs a setting also. It can only function under
government. The rule of partible inheritance was a fruitful
source of dispute. It multiplied heirs. It lodged in the kin
those provisions for wardship and dower which a lord
directed elsewhere. Gavelkind was the national custom of
Kent, a tenure of great men as well as small, and presented
problems beyond the scope of hamlet or village, needing a
court of authority and wide resort. Such a court was the
lathe, combining upon one plane, and in one system, the
threefold functions of shire, hundred, and manor, which
prevailed among the Saxons. The lathe court, as we see it
at Milton or Wye, is a court of the custom of gavelkind. It
enforces the service of gavelkind[1] and is the court for the
process of gavelate,[2] by which, in the last resort, the lord
may have forfeiture when he can get no service. In return,
it enforces those customary rules which exist for the benefit
of the gavelkinder. It supervises dower and wardship, and
particularly it watches over the interests of the tenant *infra
aetatem*, who is in the wardship of his kin. If the guardian
wastes the inheritance he will be presented and forced to
make it good. If he fails to do so the court may revoke the

[1] P.R.O. Court Rolls, Portf. 181. 74 (Milton): 'Tenentes regis qui tenentur
claudere contra boscum Castanearum et non clauserunt. Prior de Ledes. Ideo
distringitur'; ibid. 182. 1: (Wye) 'In jugo Bissop deficiunt ij perticate arure ad
Purificationem.'

[2] Ibid. 181, 74. 'Tenementum quod fuit Willelmi Tebburd in Scapeya . . .
capiatur in manu regis pro relevio et pro secta ad duas laghedayes.'

wardship and lodge it with the bailiff of the lathe.[1] The lathe is the venue of actions for real property in gavelkind. The *placita terrae* are tried in the honour court, whereas in the body of the county they would go before the shire court or the eyre as replacing the lathe. In the Milton court rolls these are freely interspersed among the other pleas, while from Wye we have the record of the fines made before the Abbot's seneschal preserved among the memoranda of the Augmentation Office.[2]

If it were possible to draw the line of division which the status of villeinage forces upon us in the Midlands, we should have to say that the lathe court as seen at Wye and Milton is essentially a court customary since it deals with the *minutiae* of tenant right. It is, however, this and much more. The lathe in Kent is, as we have already pointed out, an unspecialized court, and the custom of gavelkind covers not only tenure but every relation of life. Thus the incidents and rules of tenure are enforced in its courts indiscriminately with the greater offences of violence. The lathe tries the three ancient pleas of the Crown of Kent. It is a general court, customary, civil, and criminal. Its rolls record not only such justice as we are used to call customary, but, passing through the lesser pleas of transgression, trespass, and assault, rise to the highest, bloodshed, hamsoken, and robbery.[3]

There can be no question that these pleas of the medieval rolls recall the remote past. The new justice, such royal pleas as are of Norman growth, are beyond the compass of Wye or Milton. They have been devised since their franchise hardened to finality. But this mingling of the high justice and the low is stamped as the ancient jurisdiction of the lathe by the earliest charters which convey immunity from its court. The nobles of the eleventh century knew

---

[1] Ibid.: 'Tenementum filiorum et heredum Marie de Burdeston quod Willelmus atte Children habet in custodia capiatur in manu regis pro vasto et destruxione que Willelmus fecit in eodem.'

[2] P.R.O. Excheq. Augm. Off. M.B. 493.

[3] P.R.O. Court Rolls, Portf. 181. 74: (Milton) 'Willelmus le Mowere querens . . . contra Nicholaum Garsteyn de placito de hamsokne'; ibid. 182.1: (Wye) 'Gocele presentat quod Thomas Ruet percussit et extraxit sanguinem de Rogero atte Ware. Gualterus de Godetegh versus Henricum de Godetegh de placito baterie.'

freedom from the king's courts and the right to try hamsoken, grithbrice, and forsteal as convertible terms.[1] These, the highest pleas of the lathe under the Confessor, were precisely that justice which its court enjoys according to the surviving rolls. The lathe courts, and with them the courts of the great immunities, preserved the categories of justice as they were before the Norman Conquest, and entertained the whole custom of Kent. We may take it that for the common man, as for the noble, the lathe stood for every aspect and degree of right. Its court was the common moot of the province, wherein all his wrongs were righted, his tenure and inheritance maintained, his service enforced, and the highest offences against the king punished. Where shire, hundred, and manor divided the field of Wessex law, the lathe was the common field of Kentish custom.

To Norman eyes, all this might look like a confusion of laws. For us, it is the key to final understanding of the relation of lathe and folk. We have seen that the whole tenemental map of the gavelkind was determined by the lathe, that the sulung was the fraction of which the lathe was the whole, but we have not yet explained the obligation that this assessment was designed to meet. What primitive rent and service were the sulungs cut out to render, for something of the sort was certainly exacted from the earliest times?[2] Not the dues of the manors. The nature of the cadastre precludes them. The Danegeld is the only render to which we are used to according a public status in the Dark Ages, and the sulungs are older than the Danegeld. The dilemma is complete if we think in the Norman and Saxon terms to which we are used. But if we turn to the usage of the Kentish courts a solution is not far to seek. To the judges of the lathe the matter of custom is neither private nor public; great pleas and little, crime, transgression, peasant tenure and peasant service, all are undifferentiated, triable alike 'as the Kentish judges shall decide'. And this, surely,

[1] D.B. i. 1 a: 'Excepta terra S. Trinitatis et S. Augustini et S. Martini et exceptis his Godric de Burnes et Godric Carlesone et Alnod Cilt etc. . . . super istos habet rex forisfacturam de capitibus eorum tantummodo. Et de terris his Goslaches et Bocheland etc . . . habet rex has forisfacturas Handsocam Gribrige Foristel.'

[2] *Cart. Sax.* 194 (A.D. 759–65): 'Aeslingaham terram aratrorum xx . . . et cum omni tributo quod regibus inde dabatur.'

is the light in which we must see the hidation and its renders. If the lathe court combines the functions of shire and manor, if, being a high court, it yet adjudicates on peasant custom and enforces peasant service, it is because the dues of the free man were from the beginning quasi-manorial in form and public in theory, because gafol, precariae, and averagia, private dues in feudal law, were the king's farm from his folk in the days before it became hard to think in any but feudal terms, and so the failure to fence the king's woodland was as public a cause as robbery. It is reasonable, indeed, to suppose that the solution lies beneath our eyes, that the gavel-kind renders which are so uniform throughout the kingdom, and which have been wrested into chaos by private lordship, were once services to the royal capitals about which the sulungs make a formal pattern, that the line of Hengist maintained itself by the same natural fiscal economy as did the princes of Wales and the Anglian kings of Northumbria, and that the free folk of the provinces lost no trace of free-dom thereby.

Indeed, we are not left to conjecture. The *villae regales* have just such outliers in gavelkind as have the manors, the same in structure, the same in service. Their outland hamlets lie far and near about the lathe, witnessing to a time when no thegn or abbot came between the king and his folk. At Sutton an archipelago of hamlets covers half the lathe. The parishes of Sutton and Dartford comprise some 30 square miles of intermixed gavelkind and inland. Beyond this, Wilmington, Combe, Cranstead, Chislehurst,[1] Gilde, Grandi-sons, Portbridge, Bicknors, Stone Hill, Rowhill,[2] were all dependent tenures, owing suit, gafol, and customs, or assized rent for such, to the Sutton court at Dartford. At Faver-sham, in a compotus of the reign of Henry VIII, there still lie in to the curia rents of gavelkind from Boughton, Sellinge, Hernhill, and Dunkirk in Boughton Hundred, and from Harty, Ore, Faversham Within and Without, Graveney,[3] Baddlesmere,[4] Luddenham, Langton, and Goodnestone in

---

[1] P.R.O. *Inq. p.m.* C. Hen. III, File 24 (6) and *Cal. Inq. p.m.* 4 Edw. III, p. 223.
[2] P.R.O. *Inq. p.m.* C. Edw. I, File 71 (22).
[3] Ibid., C. Hen. III, File 41 (15).
[4] Ibid., C. Edw. I, File 101 (3).

the hundred of Faversham. The outland of Faversham is a network of hamlets disposed at random over most of the pre-Conquest lathe.

These are fragments, remaining after feudalism has done its work of disintegration. The lathe of Milton by Sitting-bourne has come down to us with its ancient structure sub-stantially intact. Subordinate tenures have, indeed, been created there, but no more than enough to show us the channels by which private ownership has been eating into the lathes in the last years of the Saxon dispensation. The natural articulation is still complete. In the time of the Confessor only 16⅛ out of 80 sulungs of outland had passed into private hands. Of these, Sidgar held 7½ at Newington, but they were in gavelkind, for the de Lacys still paid gavel-kind rent from them to Milton in the fourteenth century.[1] The evidence for tenure in fee in Milton lathe vanishes on examination and reveals the 7½ sulungs of Newington as normal outland gavelkind.[2] As to the second tenure, Hugh de Port's 8⅝ sulungs in Tunstall, Upchurch, Tonge, and Steepdown, the Survey itself is more explicit. Part of it, like Sidgar's, was gavelkind in 1066—*de istis solins quos hugo de port habet tenuit Osuuard v ad gablum.* The remaining 3⅝ had been gavelkind in the recent past—*Osuuard . . . abstulit villanis regis.*[3] The process of development here is evident. Osuuard, the sheriff of the Confessor's later writs,[4] had used his office to build up an estate in the lathe of Milton, partly by farming the outland to himself at the standard rate of gafol, and partly by ejecting the gavelkinders forcibly from their tenements. Imposing as the Norman feudalism of Kent may appear, it is here built upon recent foundations. The whole of these 80 sulungs were gavelkind in the reign of the Confessor, and gavelkind which stood in a tenemental relation to the curia of Milton.[5] Its service, which we can

---

[1] P.R.O. *Inq. p.m.* C. Edw. II, File 97.
[2] *B.B.* i. 283: 'sicut alie terre sullyngate in patria.'
[3] D.B. i. 9 a.   [4] *Cod. Dip.* DCCCLIV.
[5] *Inquisitiones post mortem* show gavelkind tenements of Milton in Shorne (C. Hen. III, File 16 (11)), Goodnestone (C. Edw. II, File 17 (7)), Tunstall, Bredgar, Milstead (C. Edw. II, File 10 (3)), Tonge (C. Edw. I, File 123 (8)), Sheppey (C. Edw. I, File 61 (13)), Milstead (C. Edw. I, File 68 (10)), Stokebury and Hartlip (C. Edw. I, File 88 (10)), Swanton (*Cal. Inq. p.m.* vii. 131).

reconstitute from Domesday and the court rolls, is that of gavelkind everywhere, gafol, food rents, minor manual services, average,[1] the fencing of the wood and demesne,[2] the maintenance of the dykes and drains against the sea. The outland of the *villae regales* bears, and apparently always has borne, the basic incidents of gavelkind custom *sicut terre sullyngate in patria*.[3]

If this theory of the slow break-up of the lathes is sound, we should be able to detect it in progress. Of the twelve or thirteen provinces into which the kingdom was once divided, Milton alone preserves its tenemental unity. Ethelbert's successors installed the churches in many royal towns, and for their endowment stripped others of whole countrysides, land, service, and jurisdiction. Their very generosity preserved the lathes instead of destroying them, for it perpetuated the system in private hands. Canterbury came to hold lathes and portions of lathes which it governed upon the old royal plan, and these are the manors of the surveys. The Archbishop, at Wingham, still received the dues of 40 sulungs. St. Augustine had 48 in Thanet and 30 at Norborne, Christchurch 17 at Adisham. These assessments were considerable fractions of provinces, and stood for an even greater real acreage. The lathe of Eastrey fell almost unbroken into the hands of the Church. In 1066, however, it was shared as to 65 sulungs between the Archbishop, his monks of Christchurch, and his knights, lying in three principal manors, Wingham, in demesne, and Eastrey and Adisham belonging to Christchurch. The lathe, we should say, had been broken up and manorialized. On closer examination, on the contrary, we find that the division is superficial, and that the matrix remains. The assessment is provincial and not manorial, a uniform sulung of 200 acres throughout the lathe, and the ancient gafol which the lathe owed is perpetuated at the uniform rate of a penny an acre *in media Quadragesima*.[4] The gafol, moreover, as becomes a provincial tax, is not paid to the courts of the manors.

[1] D.B. i. 147: 'De novem solins de Middeltone . . . xxviij pensae caseorum et dimidia et lviij solidi de gablo . . . et de his ix solins reddebat Sigar apud Mildetone averam.' Cf. P.R.O. Excheq. Augm. Off. M.B. 27, f. 16 a.
[2] P.R.O. Court Rolls, Portf. 181. 74.   [3] B.B. i. 283.
[4] Library of the Dean and Chapter of Canterbury, Reg. J, ff. 34 a, 39 a.

Eastrey and Adisham receive only *redditus, novae assisae*, and the like, from new tenements, or innovations from the old, such as *dona* and *mala*. The gafol of the sulungs goes out of the manor and is paid at Canterbury.[1] For this reason the general valet of the Exchequer Domesday is analysed into gafol and firma in the Domesday Monachorum.[2] The courts of the manor take no profit from the gafol, which is still organized on the basis of the lathe.

The hold which the *villae regales* maintain upon their ancient dues in an age of feudalism, is even more remarkable in the smaller manors held by laymen. John granted the Archbishop leave to create such tenures; *quod liceat terras . . . in gavilkinde convertere in feoda militum*; but he reserved the accustomed forinsec dues, *ita tamen quod nichilominus redditus denariorum . . . reddatur integre de terris suis sicut prius, et xenia, averagia et alia opera . . . computantur in redditu denariorum.*[3] To be lord of a manor was not enough to detach a man's land and tenants from the nexus of the lathe, and so there are innumerable small estates in Kent from which gafol and service go out to Milton, to Dartford, to Faversham, or to manors which, though never capitals, inherited shares of the lathe jurisdiction. Such were the manor of Langdon, held of the Abbot of Faversham *pro redditu solvendo per annum xxxvi sol. et x den. ob. et per servicium arandi et metendi in campo predicti Abbatis per annum sex acras terre*,[4] the manor of Preston, held of St. Augustine by rent of farm, suit, and 6 precariae in his demesne,[5] those of Dene and Westgate, which paid rents, in grain and money, and did averagia to the court of Thanet,[6] or the many estates surrounding Milton which, like Northwood, paid heavy rents *ballivo hundredi Regis de Mideltune pro firma eiusdem manerii*.[7] Even the knights' fees of the honour of

---

[1] Library of the Dean and Chapter of Canterbury, Reg. J, f. 35 a: 'Robertus de Fosseto de 1 acris dat gabulum sicut alii ad Cantuariam'; ibid. 35 b: 'xxviii d. ad curiam de Eastria de mala.'

[2] Ibid., Reg. C, f. 14 a: 'Adesham . . . de gablo redd. xvj lib. et xvj sol. iiij d. et valet xxx lib. de firma et c sol. de Gersuma'; D.B. i. 5 a: 'Edesham . . . modo redd. xlvj lib. et xvj solid. et iiij den. et archiepiscopo c sol. de Garsunne.'

[3] Bodl. MS., Tanner, 223, f. 35 b.

[4] B.M. MS. Harl. 1006, f. 165 a.　　　　　　[5] *B.B.* ii. 550.

[6] P.R.O. *Inq. p.m.* C. Edw. II, File 17 (7).

[7] Ibid., C. Edw. I, File 42 (12).

Folkestone were still bound to the work of *claustura*.[1] The slow, irregular process of detachment proceeds throughout the Middle Ages, while about the *villae regales*, like a melting ice-field, the lathe dwindles and breaks.

Though the link of service holds only here and there, the broken fragments which are the manors bear an enduring mark of their origin in land right and judicature. No Kentish manor is a unity in the sense in which a Midland manor is. The gavelkind may be broken from the lathe but it is never wholly absorbed into the manor. Here and there this fissure in law and history is embodied in the formulae of the surveys. The term *manerium* is restricted to the *demesne* and *inland*: the rest of the profit of the manor appears as *terra forinseca*, or under some neutral rubric, *redditus et servicia de tenentibus in gavylikende*, or the like.[2] More commonly, a curious but understandable perversion of the ordinary terms of record appears. Externally, the estate may be a manor, a knight's fee, perhaps, and yet internally there is division. Juries will not say that the whole manor is *liberum feudum*. The demesne is so, and the tenures of the inland, but the tenures of the gavelkind are not.[3] They are of the manor, but not of the frank tenement, and so we get a verdict which is bad in common law but good in custom, a manor *per feudum loricae* of which the major portion is not in the fee of the lord. The trend of these varying formulae is not to be mistaken. It is that of a constant effort to evade the dilemma presented by that foreign constitution of the manor, in which there is land in demesne and land in service, but both are in the fee of the lord. In Kent the real division cut across the body of the tenantry. The inland was *de feodo domini* and yet held by tenants, the outland was held by tenants in their own right, folk-right. For this reason the specialized use of *frank fee* was evolved to cover only the

[1] Ibid., C. Hen. III, File 29 (1).

[2] Ibid., C. Edw. I, File 1 (1): (Bolebrook, Sussex), 'Manerium tenetur in capite de Willelmo de Worth per servicium x s. et terra forinseca tenetur de Willelmo Wastel, heredibus Henrici de Harefeld, etc. per servicium xj s. iiij den. ob.'

[3] Ibid., C. Edw. I, File 101 (1): (Hougham.) 'Dicunt eciam quod sunt ibidem tenentes pertinentes ad liberum feudum, videlicet Petrus de Chelewartone, etc. . . . qui tenent xv acras waracres terre . . . Dicunt eciam quod sunt ibidem tenentes in gavylekende quorum Johannes Shenel', &c.

land *in manu domini* and the inland tenures whose property lay with the lord, an illuminating testimony to the power of the common lawyer to obscure the course of history. Only Kentish terms could really express the law of Kent. The simple antinomy of inland and outland served its turn perfectly, since it pointed to the separate streams of origin of the two tenures in lathe folk-right and alodial property. That is the native formula, which was found before the Conquest,[1] and persisted to the end in the forms of private record.

This flaw in the strata of Kentish feudalism determined the nature of private jurisdiction. Like their land-right, the courts of the Kentish honours were dual. The gavelkinders, when they were cut off from access to the lathe, carried their judicial personality with them and constituted a court, new in ambit but the same in essence, upon the soil of the immunity. The courts of those who secured immunity from lathes were themselves lathes. So Bromley breaks away from its immediacy to the Crown with *eall thæt læðe thæt thereto lið*.[2] It makes little difference that these courts become private, or in some cases are graded as hundreds when the lathe has been forgotten. Their pleas are the same in their pre-Conquest charters,[3] in Domesday,[4] in the *Quo Warranto* returns,[5] and in the rolls of their own courts. Wye, Eastrey, Wingham, Minster, Lewisham,[6] Norborne, keep the lathe pleas. As they keep the ancient pleas, so they keep the accustomed suit. They are not manor courts. The name of lathe still clings to them, at least in their biennial law-days. Sandwich *est laeth et hundredum in se ipso*,[7] the Prior of Christchurch still claims exemption *de lastis hundredorum*,[8] and exacts *secta de lasto*[9] from his tenants. Often these courts rank as hundreds and claim suit from land not in the barony of their lord. At Adisham the gavelkind tenants are grouped and their services estimated according to the borghi or

[1] *Cart. Sax.* 208. [2] *Cod. Dip.* MCCLVIII.

[3] Ibid. DCCCCIX: Grithbreche et hamsocne et forstalles.

[4] D.B. i. 1 a: Handsocam Gribrige Foristel.

[5] *Plac. de quo Warr.*, p. 318.

[6] P.R.O. Court Rolls, Portf. 181. 47.

[7] Domesday Monachorum, f. 66.

[8] *Plac. de quo Warr.*, p. 325.

[9] Library of the Dean and Chapter of Canterbury, Reg. J, f. 40 b: 'Apud Bosington j swling' tenetur libere . . . except' quod sequetur shiros et lastos.'

tithings of the hundreds.[1] For this reason, we have the curious spectacle of precariae and rents of the outland of Wye being enforced in a hundred court of Wye before men of the baronies of Boulogne, Perche, Say, Crevequer, Clare, and Warin fitz Gerold. In jurisdiction, as in tenure and in service, we return to the same antinomy of inland and outland. The manor never really absorbs the sulungs which it has torn from their provincial setting.

Since it cannot capture and avail itself of the lathe jurisdiction the manor must set up house for itself. Much of every great manor, such land as is under new tenure, the inland, cotland, and other fee of the lord, is subject to a new, a secondary court, which arises from that power to set up a court baron which is of common feudal right. Beside their courts of immunity they set up halimotes, inhalimotes, *curiae inmannorum*.[2] At Wye there is a *Curia de Wy*, which writes its record upon the dorse of the roll of the *Hundredum de Wy*[3] and entertains the causes of the inland, and such as arise from forinsec contracts between the abbot and the gavelkinders. At Minster, the capital of Thanet, there is an *uphalimote*[4] or *outhalimote*, for the *sulungs*, an *inhalimote* for *immanni* or tenants *extra sulingis*.[5] The hundred court, or other court of immunity held in virtue of the old and chartered exemption from the lathe, is the court of gavelkind *par excellence*, the court where the ancient services of the custom are enforced and where gavelate is pleaded. Here the gavelkind appears by its borhsealdors *de tribus septimanis in tres septimanas*, and *per omnia capita* at the two great law-days of the liberty. Inland and outland, lathe and manor, never

---

[1] Ibid., Reg. C, f. 16 b: 'Nomina tenencium Borgh' de Adesham quantum tenent et quantum debent . . . Swlinglonde, Cotyngton c acre . . .'

[2] *B.B.* i. 19: 'Redditus de In Halimot de Menstre'; Bodl. MS. Tanner 223, f. 49: Incurtland at Wrotham is unfree land; *B.B.* i. 431: 'Pro dimidia terra de coteria . . . sequentur curiam inmannorum' (Norborne).

[3] P.R.O. Court Rolls, Portf. 182. 1.

[4] *B.B.* i. 59: 'Inquisicio de huphalimot de xlv sullingis et dimidio . . . sunt preterea v sullingi et l acre in eodem halimoto.'

[5] Library of the Dean and Chapter of Canterbury, Reg. J, f. 36 a: 'dicit quod non debet sequi halemot cum aliis extra swling' ' (Eastry); Thorne, 2140; *B.B.* i. 78: 'xviij sulin pertinentes ad curiam except terra inmannorum' (Norborne). So at Minster Solomon de Chanuz does three-weekly suit from his gavelkind to the *curia de Menstre*, but for his other land suit to the *curia de Incurt*; P.R.O. *Inq. p.m.* C. Edw. I, File 108 (4).

come together even in the sphere of jurisdiction, where the pressure of feudalism must have been most constant and most heavy.

The meaning of this crossing of the normal lines of suit and service is not to be mistaken. The working compromise of the Norman manor is clearly a patchwork of two systems, different in origin and typical of two different epochs. The outland followed the lathe in the remote past when it had no lord but the king, and it continued to do so by the prevalent law of inertia, when the lathe passed to Battle, to the Archbishop, or St. Augustine, indifferent to the fact that a second economic and judicial estate had grown up about the curia and its demesne. The gavelkind and the alod are forced into intimate contact by feudalism, and the Normans find it convenient to call their association a manor, but the two lands, the two tenantries, the two lordships, are never fused into a united whole. Alod and gavelkind arose in the primitive land-law of the Jutes and set up a conflict of customs, services, and jurisdiction which the feudal law of the Middle Ages never completely reconciled.

Gavelkind is determined in its rules of succession by birthright and not seignorial right; it is non-manorial as to a part of its service, and that the oldest and most characteristic. It is not necessarily conferred by the gift of the manor. It cannot be conveyed by sub-infeudation. Where a court of lathe-immunity is held, its jurisdiction is by preference exercised in that court rather than in the halimote which is the court of the alod. All these facts point plainly to the emanation of lordship over gavelkind from the superior and pre-existing unit of the lathe.

This has been a long and tedious inquiry, but the task has been an intricate one—to release by the tracing of each separate thread of custom all that the men of the earliest English settlement understood by one phrase, 'the folk', which held for them the meaning of all society and of the duties and possibilities of each individual life. I know no better proof than their use of this one word that the state which we have been examining was the vigorous inheritor of centuries of tradition, that it was one of the great phases of civilization. From the sixth to the eighth century the word qualifies every point of status, every obligation, all power and privilege; *folk-right, folk-moot, folk-judges, folk-king, folk-land, folk-free, folk-worthy*. All custom is informed and determined by this one principle, so evident then, so hard to grasp now, when the word has been emptied of its strength and tainted with false antiquarianism.

Folk-right runs through every vein of the system we have been describing. Feudal right has no real place there. Land-right does not convey lordship, or conveys it feebly and with permanent limitations. Birthright,. the right conveyed by blood, gives the family and the individual his freedom and his land, determines his course of tillage, surrounds the homestead with a hedge of legal peace like that of lord or king, carries the poorest freeman into the public life of the moot. From this basis in the group of folk-free kinsmen all society rises as by the natural growth of a physical body. Family holding or partition, whichever predominated, equally precludes the growth of large agrarian groups, and protects the common man from that economic lordship which flourishes on monopoly of wood and waste. Equally, it enforces the free sharing of the unbroken mass of the forest. The recognition that inheritance is of folk-right preserves the vitality of the folk-moot, by making it a place of general resort. It assures it a wide ambit of jurisdiction, since it is not village by-law, but the custom of the folk, which is in question. The provincial unit forms itself naturally, as large and no larger than will permit the country-side to discharge its three-weekly suit conveniently. The lathe, in fact, is an embodied folk. Howaraland,[1] Mer-scuuare,[2] Caestruuara,[3] are synonyms for the regio of the charters which show that the folk rather than the land still hold the imagination.

Just as certainly, equality of freedom determines the forms of government. Kingship, once adopted, must be maintained. It is maintained in the natural economy of a simple age by dues of corn, food-rents, and the like, the natural renders of the countryside, perhaps from the first by rents of money; but the status of the folk is so secure that

---

[1] Saxon schedule of the Rochester bridge-work; Lambarde, p. 344.
[2] *Cart. Sax.* 214.   [3] Ibid. 199.

even manual service is natural and unobjectionable. It will take centuries of feudalism to breed the fancy that such taxes impair the freedom of the giver. The king, then, receives his farm as an equal tax upon the folk, and since natural forces have given a rough equality to the divisions of the state, an equal render falls upon the provinces. The king's town, with its reeve, is the inevitable outcome of a kingship endowed with land and the *firma patriae*. The lathe is the equally inevitable outcome of the king's charge of enforcing justice, and the need of a free population for an open and strong court of folk-right.

The lathe, then, seems to me to be the natural embodiment of the preconceptions of society which prevailed when the folk dominated all ideas about the state. Its age may well have been a long one. It is, at least, impossible to deny that Tacitus saw something of this kind in the Germania of the first century, and it is easier to suppose it to be the system of Hengist and Aesc than to imagine some Napoleonic innovator working a revolution unrecorded in the two dark centuries which followed them. Custom is not changed in such a way. Indeed, we first see it at the end of its unchallenged florescence. In 724[1] the first charter, and that suspect, vouches for the lathe. Fifty years later Offa is making the first serious encroachments upon folk-freedom with the Mercian thegnages with which he studded the valleys of the Cray and Medway. To all appearances we are here at the very base and origin of the oldest of English kingdoms.

[1] *Cart. Sax.* 141.

II

THE JUTISH SOUTH-EAST

IT may be conjectured that a civilization so distinctive and
so lasting can hardly have begun upon the narrow plat-
form of a single county. Indeed, the archaeological progress
of the last thirty years has removed its rivals from the field,
discrediting the West Saxons as a primitive power in Hampshire and showing them as later comers by way of the Wash
and the Thames. Even if we recognize a Saxon state in
Sussex entering by way of the Channel in the fifth century
(and, though the South Saxon annals of the Chronicle are of
poor repute, the evidence of custom points to a Saxon settlement along the western half of the Sussex coast), there will
still be room for a kingdom of Hengist far larger than the
Kent of the Heptarchy, nor does a strict reading of Bede
show anything against it.

I have little doubt, indeed, that a system like that of the
Kentings exercised a strong influence at one time or another
at least as far west as the Hampshire Avon, and that this
civilization, which the south-east held in common, preceded
the coming of the main stream of the Saxons. It would be
useful to have a name for these earlier settlers, though it is
dangerous to talk in terms of race, and, in the sense in which
it still seems to be allowable to speak of Angles and Saxons,
I should be inclined to adopt the name of Jutes for the
earliest inhabitants of the south-east. It carries the tradition
of identity between the people of Kent and southern Hampshire, it may be taken, if so desired, to stand for community
of custom, without committing us to purity of race, and it
does not necessarily denote a people from the Cimbric
Chersonese.

These Jutes take no small place in the amalgam of peoples
that went to make up England. There is an idiom in the
antiquity of the four south-eastern counties which is not
Saxon, even if it be not racial. With a varying intensity in
its hold upon the common life, and under various names, a
provincial system, such as governed and exploited Kent, did

prevail beyond the bounds of the Kentish kingdom, whereof one example will serve to show what may lie beneath the traditional Saxonism of the south. I have never heard it questioned that the most easterly province of Sussex, the rape of Hastings, was anything but Saxon. Yet, if we probe only a little way beneath the surface, it is not a Saxon land, but a province of Cantia Irredenta that we find, a Kentish lathe, complete in whole and members, the double of its eastern neighbour of the Lymenewara.

Perhaps the simplest proof of the Kentish affinities of Hastings is to be found in its hidation. The hide of this and other parts of Sussex has given rise to controversy because its lowest fraction is a smaller virgate than that of Wessex, ranging between 10 and 20 acres,[1] of which 8, instead of the usual 4, go to make the hide. The explanation of this anomaly seems to me to be a simple one. We have here a mixture of two assessments, Kentish and Saxon. The ground-plan, the plan of the peasant tenements, is a relic of a system of Kentish virgates, many of them held in gavel-kind, of which 16 go to the sulung,[2] each containing on the average perhaps a dozen acres. The *magna wista* of which we hear, and of which 2 made the hide, would be the Kentish jugum, present here as in eastern Surrey.[3] At some epoch the Saxons have conquered the Hastings, and have re-enumerated the larger units of the geld according to their own notation, by which 2 hides go to the sulung,[4] and 8 of these Kentish virgates to the hide. They have left the real tenements, the small virgates of the peasant tenure, as they stood. To have done otherwise would have been to have disturbed the whole system of tenure and service. In the days of the Confessor, Hastings rape contained 160 hides, omitting the hides of the Weald which were geldable elsewhere with their parent manors. Evidently, this was once an 80-sulung unit, the pair of the Lymenewara. The virgate

---

[1] The small virgate is generally common in the east of Sussex; P.R.O. Rentals and Surveys, Roll 675: Willingdon, 16–20 acres; Excheq. Augm. Off. M.B. 56, f. 269 a: Bletchingdon, 11½ acres; B.M. MS. Harl. 1761: Eastrop, 14 acres, Westrop, 12½ acres, Hodeston, 12 acres.

[2] 1 sulung = 4 juga = 16 virgates. Custumals of Battle Abbey, p. 134.

[3] At Petley the wista was of 48 acres; *Chron. de Bello*, p. 19.

[4] *Cart. Sax.* 341 (A.D. 812).

would stand at its accustomed Kentish ratio of 16 to the sulung, until the coming of the Saxon hide split each sulung into 2, and created a unit of 160 hides with the apparent anomaly of a hide of 8 virgates. Merely to state the hidation[1] of the south coast provinces in succession is to see that Hastings is the last of the lathes of Kent, rather than the first of the rapes of Sussex.

It is natural to expect that a Kentish basic assessment should be accompanied by other Kentish features. In fact, until late in the Middle Ages, much of the tenure of the rape was partible and of the hamlet form with which we are familiar in Kent. Named, bounded, and self-supporting tenements, held by groups of socii, were knit into straggling manors of the federative type by suit and service like those of Kent,[2] and in earlier times these tenures were actually recorded as gavelland, and the soil was classed, according to the Kentish division, as *inland* and *outland*. According to a charter which the Lambeth text 1212 dates in 772, Barnhorn, Writtlesham, Ibbanhurst, Crowhurst, Great Ridge, Guestling, Blackbrook, and Icklesham were all under gavelkind.[3] Moreover, not only was the groundwork Jutish, but the Kentish provincial frame was there to keep it together. The rape court of Hastings was called the Lathe of Hastings, the hidation was of 80 sulungs, and the plan of the common forest, by which the manors enjoyed their outlying pastures in the Weald, was the same as that of Kent. In 1086 the weald of the Hastings still survived in the hundred of Hailesaltede with its limbs of manors in the coastal plain, the Dallington forest of the Middle Ages. Nothing could make a stronger contrast with the unitary manor and the open field. Little in this Jutish province has changed, except that its Saxon masters have forgotten the native terms of tenure,

[1] Wyewara 80 sulungs, Lymenewara 80 sulungs, Hastings 80 sulungs or 160 hides, Pevensey 640 hides, Lewes 640 hides.

[2] P.R.O. Excheq. Augm. Off. M.B. 56, f. 1 (Glossam in Beckley): 'Johannes Ludlegh, Simon Watte et socii sui tenent diversas terras et tenementa de tenura virgate terre vocate Ludleghisyerd, que quidem virgata jacet in parochia de Bekle in hundredo de Bello et in burgo de Glaseye per metas et bundas subscriptas.'

[3] *Cart. Sax.* 208: 'þis synd þaera . . . land gemera þaer inlandes into Bæxþarena lande . . . þonne syndon þa gavolland þas ut landes.' Whether we accept 772 as the date for the *gemera* in this document or no, it is certainly a sound transcript of a charter of early date.

and have brought the larger units of the hidation into line with their own cadastre. Yet, small as the change has been, it has sufficed to conceal the real affinities of the Hastings until the present day.

The Hastings show that we need not accept the apparently solid front of Saxon England too seriously. The Saxons had achieved a political supremacy by the time when annalistic history began, and they told the story of the past in the light of England as they knew it, but there is nothing in Gildas, Nennius, or Bede to compel us to follow them. Since 1915 we have been in possession of a general survey of peasant tenure in the south-east which can hardly be bettered,[1] though minor adjustments which throw light upon the general scheme may be made at this point or another. It is a fair judgment from Dr. Gray's material to say that nothing emerges in the basic agrarian plan of southern England between the border of Hampshire, the Thames valley, and the line of the Sussex Downs to make it difficult to suppose that the whole of this area was once occupied by a people of uniform civilization and roughly uniform peasant custom. Within these bounds, as Dr. Gray's map shows, but one area of common fields and nucleated villages is found, the manors of the plain of west and central Sussex, which begin at the outflow of the Cuckmere River, and fill the belt between the Channel and the Downs until they approach the central body of Saxon village life in Hampshire, but leave the whole north of the county to the hamlet.

Upon the plane of the field system alone it is unlikely that these results will ever be seriously challenged. But the field map of the south-east is not in itself a sufficient guide to the distribution of systems of government. The field forms of part of this area are curiously neutral. In the west of Surrey they show a chaotic severalty which, while it puts out of question any development from three-field cultivation, is far less regular than the simpler hamlet form with which we have become familiar in Kent and eastern Sussex. It is clear that it is not Saxon, but at the same time it is too irregular to be used as positive evidence of the equally well-defined system of the Jutes. Agriculturally it is a no-man's-land lying

[1] H. L. Gray, *English Field Systems*.

between the two systems. In east Surrey, on the other hand, Dr. Gray has found a very marked approximation to the tenement forms of Kent, 'a tendency of virgates in that region to lie in a few parcels, or even in a single parcel. They begin, indeed, to take on somewhat the aspect of the Kentish juga'. So far west as Ewell an example of hidation by the Kentish jugum is found, and gavelkind *eo nomine* appears in the south-east of the county at Pattenden and elsewhere. The agriculture of east Sussex and east Surrey blend imperceptibly into that of Kent, but, taking the area of the south-east as a whole, the field map alone is too indefinite to give rise to sharply defined conclusions as to national boundaries.

If we turn to other sources of evidence, to peasant custom, to the use of the forest, to hidation, the picture begins to clear. Over a large area of this south-eastern country there show, only a little way below the surface, the outlines of a provincial system which clearly derives from the Jutish side of the cultural watershed between Jute and Saxon.

It may, perhaps, be thought that the case of the Hastings is that of a frontier province, an exception and recorded as such in the eleventh century:[1] but the matter is not so simple. The influence of Jutish custom is not exhausted if we do no more than move the racial boundary westward to include the Hastings in the cultural area of Kent. We come to no clear line of demarcation there. The past unity of the Hastings and Kentings is most clearly shown in their hamlet tenements and in the assessment of these upon the Kentish plan. The hamlet and the 8-virgate hide together form a double bond with Kent which we can hardly break, since it holds both in the agrarian plan and in government, and spans the whole gamut of custom between the soil and the king. The same system that cut out the hamlets also assessed them for the public fisc, presumably for that of a Kentish king or viceroy, and the hamlet is not confined to the Hastings, but extends well to the westward in Sussex and is not brought to a stand by any political landmark such as the north and south boundaries of the rapes. The hamlet in regular form occupies the east and the whole north of Sussex and the

---

[1] Simeon of Durham, *sub ann.* 771; *Anglo-Saxon Chronicle, sub ann.* 1011.

eastern half of Surrey. Except for a small settlement at the back of Beachy Head, there are no champion fields until we have crossed the Ouse going westwards, and the hamlet system in greater or less clarity is the foundation of Sussex agriculture throughout the north of the county, from the Surrey border up to, and at some points across, the line of the Downs. It is not clear that the 8-virgate hide existed west of the Hastings, albeit the wording of Domesday makes it possible, but the small size of the virgate tenements in many of the manors of the rapes of Pevensey and Lewes links them with Kent rather than with the normal Saxon plan. In the north and east of Sussex, therefore, we have a tenemental scheme much like that which we found among the Hastings with their underlying connexion with Kent.

The greater manors here are what we should expect Saxon landlordship, with its keener sense of landlord right, to make of a basic settlement in the Jutish form. The lord's right is not sporadic as it is in Kent. It extends over unbroken stretches of country, for the lord's right of property is in the soil and not merely *in servitio*. Legally, therefore, the manors are not archipelagos but continents. But the larger of them include whole groups of hamlets and have those same lodgements in the common weald that mark the growth of the Kentish manors from a foundation of folk-right. The Lewes manor of Malling covers the whole depth of the county with its 80 hides. It is in itself a country-side. Dichling, a royal *ham* of Alfred, retains the same build upon a smaller scale, though it is still a large estate. Its main mass stretches for 6 miles in the centre of the county from Patcham to Wivelsfield, but if we include the forest limbs, the *Pars Borealis* of the medieval surveys, 14 miles is its overall measure from north to south. Its wealden members lie in Balcombe, Lindfield, Cuckfield, and Ardinglye.[1] Seen upon the map with its hamlet tenements, its forest outliers, it would be indistinguishable from an estate of Kent. It is only in land-right that Saxon lordship has consolidated the manor to legal unity. Set aside the seigneurial freehold and

---

[1] B.M. Add. MS. 5705, f. 100 b: 'Liberi tenentes infra parochiam de Dichelinge de Australi parte . . . Tenentes liberi de boreali parte in Ardinglye . . . infra parochiam de Lindefeld . . . Balcombe . . . Cuckfield.'

study only its plan as the first settlers made it, and Dichling·
is federative in the Kentish form.

Though differing in important matters from that of Kent,
the custom of the Sussex hamlet area is a very free one, very
uniform in its essentials and by no means conforming to any
imagined norm of villein custom. There was customary
recognition of the birthright, dower, in many cases of a half,
as in gavelkind, wardship of minors by the kin. Tenants had
the exceptional privilege of felling the timber upon their
land like gavelkinders.[1] The tenement was often gavelland.[2]
Inheritance was by non-partible succession of the youngest
son, and the custom came to be classed as Borough English.
Manor by manor it was much alike. It has been well said
by Mr. G. R. Corner that 'this custom prevails so much
more extensively in this county than in any other part of the
kingdom, that it may almost be considered as the common
law of Sussex'.[3] Certainly it was the common law of whole
countrysides, as the uniform custumal for the Barony of
Lewes allows us to conclude,[4] and the suggestion of basic
uniformity derived from folk-right is probably as legitimate
of Sussex Borough English as it is of Kentish gavelkind. Yet
Sussex custom does not stand in isolation. Much south
Hampshire custom is of the same nature, and in the east of
Sussex, far from standing in contrast with gavelkind, the
rules of peasant tenure tend to approximate to it. Borough
English blends imperceptibly into gavelkind towards Kent
and to the west into the freer peasant tenures of the southern
Hampshire manors.

Much of the tenure of Hastings rape is partible.[5] As we
go west ultimogeniture replaces partibility, but the tenure
is still highly privileged and carries with it the terminology
and some of the most authentic stigmata of gavelkind. The
protection of gavelate is still enjoyed,[6] and this at once points
to an actual or former freehold and right to its defence in the

---

[1] B.M. Add. MS. 5705; B.M. MS. Egerton 1967, ff. 47 b, 175 a.

[2] B.M. MS. Harl. 173, f. 68 b (Hamsey): 'j mesuagium et iiij acre terre de gave-lond.'

[3] *Sussex Arch. Coll.* vi. 164.   [4] B.M. Add. MS. 5705.

[5] P.R.O. Excheq. Augm. Off. M.B. 56, f. 1 a.

[6] B.M. Add. MS. 5703, f. 27 a (Ringmer): 'De defectu cujusdam curtilagii jacentis gavellate'; cf. also, MS. Cott. Jul. B. IV, f. 18 a.

rape court. The land may be called *gavelland* and the tenants *gavelmen*.[1] There seems to be a gradual diminuendo in which Jutish tenure loses its primitive qualities as it passes away from Kent and draws towards the earliest sources of Saxon influence: first, the partible tenure of the Hastings, which is gavelkind in all but name, then Borough English with vestiges of gavelkind privilege and terminology, finally, in the west, Borough English in its simplest form. The transition which Dr. Gray found in Surrey is present in Sussex also. There is no abrupt transition, but the nearer the Kentish border, the nearer the 'common law of Sussex' draws to the Common Law of Kent.

We need not scruple to take this as representing a true process of evolution, partly because, *a priori*, we lack even the knowledge which would warrant doubt in the matter (we know very little of early peasant customs and are prone to accept the categories of the seventeenth-century lawyer as though they were primitive classifications), and partly because this form of Borough English is very much what we should expect Saxon domination to make of gavelkind if given a few centuries of unrestricted play. Partible inheritance is a troublesome custom which would be got rid of if possible. If Saxon landlords insisted on one of the sons standing as representative for the whole tenement, they would be forced to choose the youngest, since he had the right in gavelkind to the matrix of the tenement, the *astre*, the hearth, the house-place.[2] Establish the representative right of one son in place of the partible right of all and gavelkind becomes Sussex Borough English, with wardship of the kin, dower of a half, the gavelate, but with ultimogeniture instead of partition. If a parallel is called for, there is that of the transition of thegnage tenure *in paragio* into primogeniture in the eleventh century by way of a representative status in the eldest of the peers of the tenement. The change would not have come as a violation of right or at a stroke. Rather, we might associate it with the new power

---

[1] B.M. Add. MS. 5703 (Tarring): 'De una virgata et dimidia cum uno mesuagio in Salventon ... traditis eodem Simoni hoc anno in servitium de gavelman ... quantum gavelman debet de tanto tenemento.'

[2] B.M. MS. Arundel 310, f. 97 b: 'Sauve le covert del astre al puisne.'

of bargaining which profit farming gave to the lord in the Middle Ages. An early form of seigneurial interference, and one which was probably not unwelcome, was the limitation of the right of alienation to the circle of the kin,[1] and somewhat later ultimogeniture was giving place to the ordinary rules of villeinage precisely because new tenures arose and became more important than the ancient bondage. Tenants who possessed new land before inheriting land in Borough English were required to hand on their whole succession to their eldest son.[2] By such means the extinction of the older custom in favour of a villein custom in line with that of the country as a whole might come as a condition of sharing in the new enterprise of farming the waste, and ultimogeniture could give way to primogeniture in much the same way as it had itself, perhaps, ousted partition. Many primitive rules of tenure may well have outlasted the Conquest and then have been abandoned, not long before the period of manorial record, in the age of rapid economic change which set in with the twelfth century. It is not to be forgotten that the tenure of the most easterly rape was gavelland in the eighth century and that the commonest description of the Sussex tenement in that century was the *terra tributaria*.[3]

There is, then, a wide extension of the hamlet system towards the west, which in Surrey and Sussex grows more and more Kentish, more and more Jutish, in its field-plan and custom, as we draw towards the Kentish border. The effect is very much what we should look for from a Saxon conquest of a pre-existing Jutish settlement operating, not with violence, but with steady pressure through 600 years. To back the similarity in basic custom there is everywhere in the south-east a hint of earlier provincial government. Sussex has its rapes, of which the Hastings repeats the forms of the Kentish lathe; the rest of Sussex north of the Downs has many affinities with the Hastings, and so in a less degree have eastern Surrey and southern and eastern Hampshire

[1] B.M. Add. MS. 33282, f. 315 a; Porchester.

[2] At Framfield, in Sussex, when a tenant was admitted first to bondland and later to assart, descent of the whole was to the youngest son. When admission was first to assart and later to bondland, succession was to the eldest son; B.M. MS. Egerton 1967, f. 237 a.

[3] *Cart. Sax.* 50, 64, 144, 145, 198, 212, 262.

There is the same forinsec wood-right. The denes of the Kentish manors, the *communis silva* of the lathes, are repeated faithfully in the Saxon rapes. Each has its forest, the four easternmost in Andred,[1] Arundel and Chichester, perhaps, in central areas where Arundel Park[2] and Charlton Forest now lie, and as far back as charters go grantors couple denes with *terra tributaria*,[3] thus recognizing that, as constituent parts of the rape, the manors have their right of participation in its common weald. These forests are *communis silva*, for the most part outside the fiscal body of the rape, as being ancient common waste,[4] just as the *communis silva* of Kent was outside the lathe. For this reason they were mainly ingeldable in Domesday. They have hides and virgates in the Middle Ages but many of them were for the convenience of estates management, as were those of the Kentish denes, and were *foris rapum*, supernumerary to, and not geldable in the ancient assessment. The Domesday assessment is small. The use of the Weald in Sussex and Kent, and indeed in Surrey, is essentially the same.

An identical formula is found in southern Hampshire, though there, away from Andred, the smaller woods of Bere and the New Forest lie as central masses around which the constituent hundreds are ranged and intercommon. The charters of the pre-Conquest age specify these forinsec wood-rights of the Meonwara in terms identical with those of Kent and Sussex. It is not the greatness of Andred which imposes

[1] Hastings, Dallington; Pevensey, Ashdown; Lewes, Worth; Bramber, St. Leonard's; Arundel, Arundel; Chichester, Charlton.

[2] Thus, Felpham had wood pasture in Bignor, too far south to be part of the Weald, but well within the possible radius of Arundel Forest. *Cart. Sax.* 898.

[3] *Cart. Sax.* 961 (Annington): 'þis sint þa den stopa, broc hyrst and beaddan syla and æt fyrnþan and hliþ wic and strod pic.' So Washington has denes in 'the three Crowhursts', Horsham, and Wivelsborough, names which are familiar as modern parishes in the forest—'þis synt þa den þe þær to ge byrigeaþ'; ibid. 834. The earliest charter granting denes is of East Dene in 725 'and ða dænn aerest þær scealces burna and bollanea' (Bolney Parish), &c.; ibid. 144. Cf. also ibid. 197 (Stanmer); ibid. 198 (Ferring). Cf. D.B. i. 22 b, where a group of manors in Lewes Rape have detachments in Grinstead Hd. in the Weald: Falmer, Hamsey, Barcombe, Dichling, Bevendean, Allington, Warningore, Wootton; and ibid. i. 19, where Alciston, Berwick, Ripe, West Firle, Willingdon, Chalvington, Ratton, &c. have outliers in Shoyswell Hd.; also ibid. i. 19 a, Arlington, Laughton, Waldron, and others have outliers in Hawksbury Hd.

[4] *Cart. Sax.* 898 (Felpham): 'Et in communi silva pascuale quod dicitur Palinga Schittas.'

the system, but a general custom. The Kentish *communis silva* is not Kentish only, but south-eastern, and is determined not by geography but by custom, for in western Surrey, where the manors still lay within range of Andred but Saxon custom was in the ascendant, no such use of the Weald was ever made, nor is it apparent that it was established in the purely Saxon area of western Sussex.

Miss Cam's researches[1] have shown how prevalent is the grouping of hundreds for administration, but this in itself does not guarantee an ancient provincial status. Nor is the association of a group of hundreds for the exploitation of the forest conclusive proof that the constituent hundreds formed a province for administration, though the association of such a system with the lathes of Kent and the rapes of Sussex is clear, and I do not know how the rights of the rival hundreds could have been delimited in the beginning without some provincial authority, or reconciled in practice without some such intervention as Uualhhun exercised in the Chesterwara.[2] But there are other marks of provincial identity to be reckoned with, and especially in the original build of the hidation. In Kent one of the clearest proofs of the predominance and antiquity of the lathe is the divorce of the sulungs from the contemporary reality of agriculture and lordship, and its identity with the primitive province. Such a divorce is proclaimed even more strikingly in the terminology of tenure in Sussex, south and east Hampshire and eastern Surrey than it is in Kent. In Kent the ingeldable inland and demesne and the *communis silva* of the Weald is fiscally and jurisdictionally exempt from the ancient hidation. The Latin describes it as being *extra sullingis*,[3] outside the constituent units of the lathe, and one constantly expects to come upon some such phrase as *extra lasto, foris lastum*, or *forlathe*. As far as my experience goes, this apparently

---

[1] *Eng. Hist. Rev.*, xlvii (1932), 353–76.

[2] In the eleventh century the control lay with the sheriff. D.B. i. 49 b (Acangre, Hants): 'Scira vero testatur quod non potest habere pasturam nec pasnagium de silva regis . . . nisi per vicecomitem.' Later it was exercised by the Custos of the Forests citra Trentam; B.M. Add. MS. 33, 284, f. 43. Neither of these officials existed in the ninth century.

[3] Library of the Dean and Chapter of Canterbury, Reg. J, f. 36 a: 'Dicit quod non debet sequi halemot cum aliis extra swling'.'

inevitable term does not occur in Kent, but its analogue does appear in Sussex, and, surprisingly enough, in Hampshire and Surrey also. The ingeldable of Sussex, the forest outliers of the Weald and the new land of the agricultural estates, being apart from the ancient geldable (hides, wistas, virgates) are 'outside the rape', and appear in Domesday as *foris rapum*[1] and in the later surveys as *forepeland*.[2]

The significance of this in Sussex, where the rape is a commonplace of administration, is plain enough. The rape is an organic fiscal and jurisdictional entity, a body politic having its meaning in the past of law, taxation, and government, and in no way reflecting contemporary reality. It is a state within the state, the hidated area only, and not the hundred or so square miles of land, wood, and water that lie between Ouse and Adur, Adur and Arun. The rape is an abstraction, not the land but the hidation, and as old as the hidation. Population grows and is redistributed, new land is brought into cultivation and old land falls into decay, but the rape remains as it always has been, a rigid, fiscal and legal network, gripping one acre, avoiding another, holding the same tenements *a tempore a quo non extat memoria*. There were new values to be reckoned in Domesday, and they were so reckoned, but *foris rapum*, as those of Kent were *extra sullingis*. The caprice of jurors has caused the ingeldable manorial hides to be recorded in the Domesday of Hampshire and Sussex and has omitted those of Kent,[3] but the ancient royal obligations are restricted to the ancient geldable in all alike. Custom is infinitely tenacious where liability and exemption are at stake. The antinomy of *rape* and *forrape* holds in the Conquest and throughout the Middle

[1] D.B. i. 28 a: 'Terra iii carucarum ... Foris rapum est et extra numero hidarum'; ibid. i. 17 b: 'Ipse Abbas habet in rapo suo vj hidas et dimidiam. Haec terra pro vj hidis se defendebat et dimidia fuit quieta quia foris rapum ... Adhuc est una silva foris rapum de v porcis'; ibid. i. 20: 'Ipse comes tenet in suo dominio unum villanum qui jacuit in Selescombe et tenet unam virgatam foris rapum. In Selescombe ... una virgata. Nunquam geldavit et semper fuit foris rapum.'

[2] B.M. MS. Egerton 2418, f. 31 b (Droxford): 'Ricardus Hamelyn tenet j ferling terrae foreplend'; *Crondal Records*, Hampshire Record Society, ed. F. J. Baigent (Sutton), p. 136 (Dippenhall), p. 204, (Yateley), p. 296; B.M. Add. MS. 5701, f. 122 b (Bosham).

[3] The denes of Lenham, Ickham, and other manors of Kent are hidated in manorial surveys, but these hides are not recorded in Domesday and do not bear the ancient suit and service of gavelkind.

Ages. In all essentials it is the duality of Kentish tenure under another name.

This is hardly surprising in Sussex, where the rape has survived to stamp its identity upon the great survey, but the appearance of an identical terminology in Surrey and Hampshire, where it has not, opens a wider speculation. If the rape ever existed in these counties *eo nomine*, it had faded out of the scheme of royal administration by 1066 and left no mark on Domesday. All the more remarkable is it, then, to find that the classification of land according to its liability to, or immunity from, a rape has survived in the pre-Conquest charters of east Surrey and in the post-Conquest manorial records of Surrey and Hampshire. The rape did not survive in Surrey in 1066. A hundred years earlier it did survive to the extent that it was still necessary to specify whether land transferred by charter was within the rape, or was exempt from it as being part of the ingeldable forest. The region in which Merstham lay had its denes in Tandridge,[1] in its beginnings a *weald* and in Domesday a hundred. In 947 Edred gave land at Merstham and with it two denes, Pedan hrycg and aet Lace, being *forrape*,[2] and, we cannot but conjecture, *forrape* to a *rape* in which Merstham then lay, or had lain within traditional memory.

We can, I think, see a progression in time by which the primitive provincial scheme of the south-east is slowly fading out of memory under the domination of the Saxons. In Kent it is still powerful in almost every phase of life in 1086. In Sussex it has suffered far more from manorialism than in Kent, and from manorialism in the destructive form of the small secular thegnage, but it still imposes itself upon the rubrics of Domesday. In eastern Surrey—and there is no evidence for it in the west of the county—it has ceased to determine the administrative divisions for an unknown period, but three generations earlier it is still remembered in a provincial allotment of the Weald like that of Kent and Sussex. The province has gone, but the profitable

---

[1] *Cart. Sax.* 470 (Sutton): 'Suttone . . . cum porcorum pascuis on Thene wold.'
[2] Ibid. 820: 'þis sind þa den to Mearsaetham pedan hrycg et æt lace þæt forrape.' This is confirmed by a charter of Eadgar (*Cod. Dip.* DCVI) in which Lace and Tandridge appear as *silvae pertinentes* to Beddington.

wood-right of the forest and its allocation remain. The *rape* is forgotten, but the *forrape* is remembered. Through the centuries of Saxon government the old provincial organization of the south-east is gradually sinking from the level of administration to a purely agrarian function, and in the political mind of the race from the conscious to the unconscious, till it is used mechanically to record existing immunities, with no sense of the historical institutions from which those immunities derived.

This last phase when the rape-lathe can no longer force itself upon the king's records, but works effectively in the petty affairs of country life and determines the idiom of private accounting, is excellently exampled in the manorial surveys of Sussex, Hampshire, and Surrey. So at Bosham[1] the ancient organized and hidated virgates of the village custom are *bondland*. The newer tenures of the inland are *forreplond*. In Hampshire, in the Meonwara, the hidated customary land bears the ancient gafol and the oxyeve, renders which we have seen in the gavelkind of eastern Kent. The *forreplond* is held in irregular scraps and at rent.[2] The same immunity from the older manorial service is enjoyed by the land *foris rapum* in the three western counties as is enjoyed by the land *extra sullingis* in Kent, and it suffers the same exclusion from the protection of the authentic custom of the manor. It is not hard to see that the rape had once a real meaning here, and that at some period in the past, however remote, the manors have drawn the units of a province into their structure as the manors of Kent absorbed the sulungs of the lathe. As is so often the case, the survival of a single term of peasant tenure has opened up for us a whole epoch of government.

It is possible, I think, to use this hint from manorial custom as a direct guide to past administration. The term 'forrape' leads us to two features which were vital to our understanding of the lathe, to the exploitation of the forest,

---

[1] B.M. Add. MS. 5701, f. 122 b.

[2] Ibid. MS. Egerton 2418, f. 29 b: 'Ricardus de la More et Ricardus de la More Junior tenent dimidiam virgatam terrae et reddunt de gabulo ij sol et de xvj acris foreplond xv.d.'; *Crondal Records*, Hampshire Record Society, ed. F. J. Baigent, p. 136: 'Thomas Andreu tenet j messuagium et unam virgatam terrae ... Idem tenet unam parcellam de Forreplond.'

since in one of its applications the *forrape* is the *weald*, that common wood which lies apart from the hidated area, and also to the hidation, since it is only with reference to units of assessment that the terms *rape* and *forrape* have any meaning. Of these two, contrary to what might be expected, the use of the woodland according to the lathe custom of Kent is quite as good a test as the hidation. It might be thought, on first consideration, that so simple an arrangement would be universal, but it is not. It seems to be Jutish only, and I think that if we remember the intricate and highly organized tissue of custom upon which it depended in Kent, we shall understand that it is not to be imported lightly into Saxon manorialism. In fact it is confined to that part of Surrey where Kentish affinities are most marked, to Jutish Hampshire, and to the area of the hamlet and the federative manor in Sussex, and this irrespective of whether forest is available near at hand or not. Out of some forty examples of the association of Sussex manors with forinsec wood in the weald, only two are under open-field culture. These are Alciston and Berwick, the outermost manors on the north edge of the enclave of unitary manors at Beachy Head. All the rest are either shown to be federative in medieval surveys, as are Dichling, Keymer, Falmer, and many others, or lie well within the great belt of hamlet settlement. The fact seems to be that the weald is an integral part of the Jutish provincial system, a provincial reserve of wood which must have a province to serve. A *forrape* can only exist as the pair of a *rape*, and the whole institution evolves from a particular organization by *wara*, and begins as the *communis silva* of a folk. Forinsec denes are, therefore, an extremely good test of what is Saxon and what is Jutish. Fortunately both hidation and forest-right are persistent factors in the south-east, far more persistent than administration and its courts. They cannot be changed without impinging on the interest of small men and great; consequently, where the life of provincial government has been long dead and all conscious record of it has ceased, we may still find its impress, its unconscious record, in the forest and the grouping of hides in what once were provincial outlines.

If we were to draw our map of this part of England to

demark the spheres of Jutish and Saxon influence upon grounds of agrarian and customary evidence, that is by the shape of the peasant tenement alone, we might reasonably begin our boundary by a line from Richmond southwards, dividing Surrey roughly into two halves, and from the south of this line go westward following roughly the existing boundary of Surrey and Sussex, and cutting across the south of Hampshire at the head of Southampton Water, to include the New Forest and the Meonwara. All to the south and east of this line would be Jutish, with the one exception of the Saxon coastal settlement from Chichester Harbour to Beachy Head. Such a line would be roughly true to the facts of custom, but it could not be a hard and fast one. The custom of west Surrey is too difficult of interpretation to be lightly placed in either racial scale. In southern Hampshire, in so far as evidence is available, elements of both customs seem to be present. There are hamlet settlements between the Portsdown Hills and the sea,[1] but near them is the great unitary manor of Porchester.[2] Meon Stoke exacts service of week-work from its villeins and seems to be under open fields.[3] Titchfield has much land in severalty and reproduces the indefinite tenures of west Surrey with some tendency to take the hamlet form.[4] Some at least of the Winchester manors seem involved in champion farming, but their tenure is exceptionally secure and their service startlingly recalls the gavelkind of Kent.[5] Indeed, throughout this area the right of succession is rigorously respected, and Borough English is common, with privileges such as wardship by the kin.[6] If much of the Surrey tenure is neutral that of the Meonwara might well be a patchwork in which Jute and Saxon dwelt as neighbours.

With the help of our fresh criteria a decision becomes possible. Whatever may have happened in the earliest phase of the invasion, however far the peasant stock of the first comers extended, they have left recognizable traces of their government to the east and south only of our proposed line

[1] B.M. Add. MS. 33284, ff. 239, 277, &c.   [2] Add. MS. 33282, f. 283.
[3] Add. MS. 33284, f. 35 a.   [4] Add. MS. 33284, ff. 93 a, 110 a, 277 a.
[5] B.M. MS. Egerton 2418, f. 31 b (Droxford): 'Et reddit de gabulo xvd., de Oxyeve iijd. et arabit j acram.'
[6] B.M. Add. MS. 33284, f. 255; B.M. MS. Egerton 2418, f. 316.

of division, but have left them there too plainly to be mistaken.

The cadastre of Sussex, as we have already seen, is in
itself the rape, and it follows that we must look for the outline
of the cadastral scheme in the province which bears that
name, not in the township or the hundred, and find it in
Sussex in the rape, as in Kent we found it in the lathe. The
easternmost, the Hastings, is itself a lathe.[1] It carries on the
sequence of the Kentish provinces with its 160 hides or 80
sulungs. The other five, more populous and less deeply
involved in forest, embody the common principle of hidation
by eighties which characterizes the south-east, but are more
heavily burdened. Pevensey carries 640 hides, Lewes 640,
Bramber 480, Arundel 400, Chichester 800.[2] So, I believe,
in rounded numbers, the text of Domesday should be
interpreted.

The bridge province of the Hastings prepares us to find
that the hidations of the two kingdoms have something in
common, and Sussex in turn provides a link with the three
provinces of the most westerly group of Jutish peoples, the
Meonwara, the folk of the New Forest, and of the Isle of
Wight. The Meonwara, the group of hundreds east of the
Meon to the Sussex border, is an almost lineal reproduction
of the provincial form of Kent. Lying about its central
forest and confined between the river and the sea the seven
hundreds combine to make up a rounded unit of hidation,
480 hides.[3] The forest itself, Bere Forest, repeats the
Kentish Wealds. Its status as the *communis silva* of a folk
of the Meonwara is vouched for by charter as late as
A.D. 825,[4] and the attachment of its denes to the manors of

---

[1] With the Hastings we have a simple demonstration that rape and lathe are
identical with a difference of name only. The Kentings, fastening upon the
function of jurisdiction, call their province *lathe,* quasi *soke.* The men of Sussex
and Surrey, looking to the land rather than to the soke due from it, call theirs
the *rape*—the cadastre, or assessment, recalling the *reebning* or *rebdragen land* of
Denmark. (Vinogradoff, 'Growth of the Manor,' p. 264). In the Hastings the
province is proved to be patient of both interpretations. It is at once a lathe of
jurisdiction and a fiscal rape.

[2] *Eng. Hist. Rev.* xlv. 427.

[3] Ceptune 83, Mene 88¼, Ferneham 42½, Menestoch 102, Portesdone 52¼, Bose-
berg 48¼, Ticefelle 52, Warblitone (entered in the Sussex survey) 12.

[4] *Cart. Sax.* 393: 'Meonwara snade' in the metae of Droxford.

the coast appears in a charter of Alverstoke a hundred years later.[1] During the Middle Ages we are able to mark down manors from every one of the hundreds of the Meonwara as holding forinsec woods within the bounds of Bere Forest.[2] The demonstration of its weald status seems therefore to be complete. In the reign of Henry II the district of 'Mienes' still appears as a separate firma of about the value of all the royal lands in the seven hundreds *Tempore Regis Willelmi*,[3] and it seems that Meon Stoke had some sort of dominical authority over a good deal of the seven hundreds *Tempore Regis Edwardi*. Alverstoke was in Meonstoke Hundred and Titchfield was still a Meonstoke berewick in 1086. The provincial unity begins to emerge as we follow back the Meonwaras into history.

The second mainland province of the Hampshire Jutes is an equally perfect formation. Its hidation is half that of the Meonwara, 240 hides,[4] for much of it is forest. The Domesday record of hides *nunc in foresta* and pasture lost by the afforestation of William's reign shows us almost all the greater estates of the coastal fringe and the Avon valley as having forinsec wood in the New Forest,[5] and the Domesday is confirmed by the later records of Beaulieu Abbey and other manors.[6] In hidation and in its exploitation of the weald the western province can have differed little from the east.

If we turn to Surrey the record of the hidation almost

---

[1] Ibid. 865: 'And fyrð ora is on wudu to stoce and ðæt maesten is gemaene to ðam an and twentigum hidum.' If *Cart. Sax.* 1314 refers to Alverstoke we have an even earlier record: 'ðis sind ða den into Stoce. Siblingehyrst and Trowinsceadas and Rocisfald.'

[2] In Bosebergh Hd. the manors of Warblington, Middleton, Emsworth (P.R.O. *Inq. p.m.* C. Edw. II, File 16 (9)). In Chalton Hd. Chalton and Catherington (B.M. Add. MS. 33282, f. 288 and P.R.O. *Inq. p.m.* C. Edw. I, File 53 (15)). In Portsdown Hd. Portsea in Portseyewode, Copnor in Copenore Wood (B.M. Add. MS. 33281, f. 2). Cosham and Wallsworth (ibid. 33282, f. 109). In Titchfield Hd. Wickham (ibid. 33282, f. 288). Part of the forest lies in the Hundred of Meonstoke. Portsdown Hd. (*Rot. Hundr.* ii. 224).

[3] D.B. i. 38 a: £145 10s. Pipe Roll, 5 Hen. II: £130 16s. 6d.

[4] Bovere Hd. 46⅓, Egheite 36¾, Sirlei 28½, Fordingbridge 47⅞, Ringwood 15, Rodbridge 32, Rodedic 33¾.

[5] D.B. i. 38 b (Ealing): ibid. 39 a (Ringwood); ibid. 44 b (Over): 'Totum nemus hujus manerii est in foresta regis'; ibid. 46 a (Rochford): 'Silva in foresta regis.'

[6] P.R.O. Rentals and Surveys, Portf. 14, no. 54. Ringwood has wood pasture in the New Forest 'inter Militem et Armigerum', Knight's wood and Squire's wood, which survive to-day about 6 miles into the forest from Ringwood.

completely fails us. The county seems to be a round unit of
2,000 hides, 1,998¼, according to my reckoning,[1] and the
most notable feature at first sight is the marked difference
in the system between the eastern and western halves. If we
take the line of the Beverly Brook as our partition, all that
lies to the west is understandable, with some allowance, by
the traditional Saxon grouping in hundreds, half and double
hundreds of an actual hundred hides.[2] East of that line the
county contains only three hundreds of disproportionate
size, Brixton of 280, Wallington of 380, and Tandridge of
270. It is worth mentioning, though not much weight can
be laid on the fact, that these three hundreds, with the
adjacent Kentish hundreds which are themselves left over
from the assessment of Sutton Lathe, make up a round total
of a thousand. The western half of the county is indubitably
the work of Saxon assessors, while the eastern half conforms
to no system at all, but falls into divisions which may either
represent the break-up of an original province of a thousand
hides athwart the present Surrey–Kent boundary, or may
themselves be provinces which have lost their regularity, or
in fact may be the work of chance and so carry no meaning
of any historical value at all.

Disappointing as this result is, it tells us something positive. The agrarian scheme of west Surrey is too indefinite
to prove a primitive Saxon settlement there. If anything, it
is easier to reconcile with the looser system of the Jutes. But
though we may question the origin of the peasantry of west
Surrey and their custom, the build of the hundreds leaves
us in no doubt as to the source of government. At whatever
epoch we care to place the formation of the hundreds in this
part of England, it must be at a time when the line between
east and west Surrey was a real division, when it stood for
some contrast of race, law, or historical continuity so strong
that the Saxons could extend their normal administrative
plan to the middle line of the county but could not impose it
upon the east. West Surrey stands with the midland hundredal scheme in administration. East Surrey does not.

[1] Mr. H. E. Maldon puts the total at 2,002½ hides.
[2] e.g. Godley 100, Godalming 100½, Kingston 100, Effingham 48½, Copthorn
203¼, Churchfell 106.

G

It is unfortunate that we cannot take the further step and reconcile the hidation of the rest of the county with the provincial scheme of the Jutish settlement. Unless we are to take the thousand hides of the three eastern hundreds of Surrey and the four western hundreds of Kent as the administrative pair of the lathe of Sutton, the forrape of Tandridge weald no longer corresponds to any rape or lathe grouping of the hides, and there is room for two or even three rapes in these thousand hides. But though we can make nothing of the fiscal scheme as it lay in 1066, it is clear that the identity in custom with Kent and Sussex, for which the weald of Tandridge, Thenewold, stands, is confined wholly within the three most easterly hundreds of Brixton, Wallington, and Tandridge, save for two points where it is pushed forward a mile or so to the west, and that identity is very close. We have here that crystallizing of the formless severalty of Surrey tenure into the hamlet form of Kent which Dr. Gray has noticed. We have the appearance at Ewell of the Kentish assessment unit of the jugum, and gavelkind appearing in the south-east.[1] We have the rape in its complement of the forrape. Finally, we have a series of pre-Conquest charters conveying wealden denes as complements of the estates granted in the familiar Jutish formula,[2] and of all these not one falls outside the three hundreds by more than a mile, and all unite to place the denes in the weald of Tandridge. Clearly, there was here a normal relation of weald and province. There is thus a sharp division across the modern county of Surrey, leaving the Thames at Mortlake, following the line of the Beverly Brook to Sutton, and thence making south to Andred along the western boundaries of the hundreds of Wallington and Tandridge. West of that line is Saxon hidation, indefinite peasant custom, and an entire lapse of the south-eastern economy of the forest: east of it is conformity in all essentials with the economic life of Kent.

Remembering the strength of the organic relation in

[1] At Lingfield, P.R.O. *Inq. p.m.* C. Edw. I, File 48 (2).
[2] *Cart. Sax.* 820: 'þis sind þa den to Mearsaetham pedan hrycg et æt lace'; ibid. 1155 (Beddington); ibid. 1198 (Chaldon); ibid. 39 (Cheam and Banstead); D.B. i. 30 b (Ewell): 'Una dena silvae.'

which the constituents of early custom stand to each other,
the close resemblance of the hamlet tenements of Surrey,
Kent, and Sussex, the identity of the weald system in all
three counties and southern Hampshire, and the characteristic part which the weald played in the economy of the lathe
together with the survival of the rape in private record, I
believe that the early history of southern Hampshire, east
Surrey, and perhaps the predominant influences in that of
Sussex, arose out of a culture which was specifically south-
eastern and finds its least impaired survival in Kent. For
this, I think there is sound evidence. Beyond this area such
facts as have survived will not carry us, but on broad grounds
of probability it is unlikely that a Jutish settlement should
have crystallized exactly upon the frontier line of their
administrative survival as we have seen it, with its unnatural
division of Surrey and the awkward projection of Sussex and
south Hampshire along the front of the Celtic or Saxon
power. Common sense would suggest that the debatable
ground of custom, the deep Saxon salient of west Surrey and
the eastern hamlet fringe of Hampshire, must have been
occupied by a primitive invasion from the south-east, and
there is no sufficient reason to the contrary.

Upon the evidence that I have given, the result of a
fairly complete survey of the sources for Kentish institutions,
and of a more cursory one of those for Sussex, Surrey, and
Hampshire, I should be willing to conclude that the first
great phase of the English invasions was a general settlement
of England south of the Thames as far west as the Hampshire Avon, by a homogeneous people to whose survivors
in his own day Bede gave the name of Jutes. The proposi-
tion is less revolutionary than it may sound at first hearing.
The major achievement of English archaeology in the last
thirty years has been to lift the weight of the Saxon onslaught
from the Channel coast and to bring the Saxons into Britain
from the Thames and the Wash. In so far as archaeology is
a sure guide they are no longer a south-coast power, but,
with the exception of the small enclave of the South Saxons in
west and central Sussex, a people from the North Sea and the
east. The early Saxon annals of the *Anglo-Saxon Chronicle* are
deservedly discredited, and the whole of our contemporary

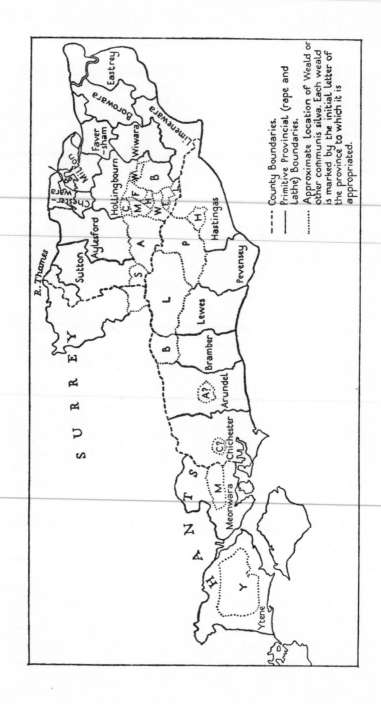

County Boundaries.

Primitive Provincial (rape and Lathe) Boundaries.

Approximate Location of Weald or other communis silva. Each weald is marked by the initial letter of the province to which it is appropriated.

picture of the invasion period, which, though it has been contradicted on several fundamental grounds, still possesses contemporary thought, is in reality based upon those annals and on nothing more. Their authority is not such as to deserve their long ages of acceptance, for they are the work of a scribe of the West Saxon dynasty, working upon the slightest of foundations, and writing for a victorious king who had made Wessex a synonym for England. The Kentish annals, which command far greater respect, place no territorial limit to the sphere in which Hengist and Aesc *fengon to rice*, and the whole trend of the Celtic sources, such as they are, is against the *Chronicle*'s record of piecemeal conquest. In Celtic story it is Aesc, Osla Gyllellvawr, who fought with Arthur at Badon, and I know no better claimant.

If, then, on the authority of the Kentish annals of the *Chronicle*, we bring Hengist and his Jutes to Britain in the middle of the fifth century and give him a substantial south-eastern kingdom, we shall not be at odds with written history. An incursion of the West Saxons into Hampshire in the middle of the sixth century is all that the credit of the *Chronicle* will bear, and from that point it is but two genera-tions to the Bretwealdership of Ethelbert. With their effec-tive occupation of northern Hampshire, we may link the Saxon conquest of west Surrey, the destruction of its Jutish administration, and perhaps some degree of settlement. The Beverly Brook would then form the north-western boundary of the Jutish power and near that time at Wibbandun Ethel-bert took his stand to meet the fresh onslaught of the Saxons under Ceawlin in 568. Meanwhile, the Channel settlement of the South Saxons would be greatly strengthened by the arrival of a new and powerful Saxon state in Hampshire and Surrey, in the face of which a government based on Canter-bury could hardly maintain its hold upon the long and narrow extension of the coastline. Hitherto the Saxon element there had been an intruder. It was never really incorporated in the provincial government of Sussex. It was shut out from the enjoyment of the national pasture reserves. The emergence of an independent kingdom of Sussex, and the severance of the western provinces from Kent, would be a natural consequence of the rise of Wessex. But by the end of the sixth century the age of migration was passed. The Jutes of east Surrey were neither massacred nor evicted. Their government was destroyed, but much of their civilization survived into the Middle Ages. In the south the Saxon onrush did not reach the Channel. The West Saxons contented themselves with their hold upon the greater part of Hampshire and turned their attention towards the Celtic principalities of the west which they broke at Deorham. The conquest of the Channel provinces of the Jutes was delayed for a century, and when it came was the work, not of the West Saxons or of the migration period proper, but of the new age of political supremacy based on the military power of settled governments. Wulfhere of Mercia, in alliance with Ethelwald, king of the South Saxons, drove out the dynasty of the Western Jutes from the Wight, placed them under the rule of Sussex, and perhaps at that time also the province of the Hastings was detached from its dependence upon Kent and added to the kingdom of Ethelwald. If so, it was at this epoch of the first Mercian supremacy, in the third quarter of the seventh century, that Kent first took on its modern boundaries, and the Heptarchy as Bede knew it came into being.

Such an hypothetical reconstruction is not to be taken literally. We have no warrant for associating the phases of decline with the traditional men and places of the *Chronicle*. Nevertheless, the speculation is worth making as a time-scale by which the submerging of Jutish England may be set against the accepted order of history. It should at least be true in essence. The story that Aella led the South Saxons into Sussex in the fifth century may well be true. Sussex is a state in which the Saxons and Jutes dwell side by side without mingling. The parallel of the Saxon enclave in the Frankish settlement across the Straits of Dover suggests itself. The form of government is Jutish—no name of any South Saxon king has come down to us for just on two centuries after the dubious figure of Aella—but the Saxons keep their social habit until they gain political supremacy. Saxon theories of lordship then begin to modify social relations throughout the kingdom. West Surrey, and such of east Hampshire as went with it, preserve the characteristics of neither people; they suggest an early conquest and at least a partial settlement, and their loss may well be placed in the days when the Saxons were still in migration. East Surrey should be the next to go; it has lost its Jutish administration, but the survival of its economic and social groundwork suggests no general settlement and carries its absorption out of the period of folk-wanderings. The generation before Ethelbert may well have seen the stabilizing of the West Saxons as a settled state, with the battle of Wibbandun as their first essay in external conquest. The Meonwara and the New Forest, clearly, are not greatly changed. The *Chronicle*'s record of the subjection of the Wight in 661 may safely be accepted, and may have brought the end of the Meonwara also. Lastly the Hastings, who, if we accept the Lambeth text of Offa's charter, were lost before 772, but preserved their Kentish institutions intact and perhaps some measure of autonomy, must have been won in some successful war waged upon Kent by Sussex, and from what we know of their history the alliance of Sussex with Mercia in 661 seems to be the one occasion when such a conquest was possible. Such may have been the course of history, at least in the broad succession of phases that reflect themselves in custom.

III

THE CONTINENTAL JUTES

THE settlement of the Iutae in Britain has a strong identity of its own. It seems to me that it is compact enough and sufficiently tenacious of its characteristics to be called racial in any sense in which the word is worth using. It is possible, of course, to define race so strictly that it is useless as an historical term. Unmixed purity of blood is impossible to establish, and if we go back far enough we shall find that every race has compromised its integrity at some time and in some degree. But still the term seems to be worth using if we are clear as to the meaning we give to it, and in virtue of its distinctive custom, and of the exceptional flowering of Kentish art in the sixth and seventh centuries, it seems right to regard the south-eastern settlement as a separate racial element among the English peoples, and one whose thousand years of life as a recognizable individuality in Britain might be expected to have some few centuries of preface upon the Continent—at least enough to enable us to link our English Jutes with one of the known races of Germany.

This task of identification would be easier if there were not already an accepted view as to the provenance of the Iutae, which claims as its sanction the authority of Bede, but which is past all quibble mistaken. That is the view that the English Jutes derived their origin immediately from Jutland. Bede tells us that the Angles came from Angulus, and that Angulus lay *inter provincias Iutarum et Saxonum.* This Angulus may be Angel, the promontory between the Trave and the Kielerhaf, though even with this as a fixed point the position of the Iutae is not clearly defined. (There were Saxons across the whole width of northern Germany from the Rhine to Mecklenburg and from Schleswig to Thuringia.) If we take Bede literally and insist on the Baltic Angel as our point of reference, the Iutae should lie on the Lübecker Bucht, perhaps on the site of the later province of Eutin, or, less probably, farther north between the Schlei and the

Eider. Even so, the identity of the provincia Iutarum with Jutland will not be established, for there is nothing in Bede to warrant the pushing of the Iutae a hundred miles to the north beyond the Königsau. That identification is based upon a similarity of names, and one which has been seriously challenged on philological grounds. If, as we equally well may, we take Angeln for the province of Engern to the west of the Weser, our Jutes will lie in Friesland, or farther south between the Ems and the Rhine. The field for conjecture is thus a wide one. Give the fullest weight to Bede's words and they do not tell us much.

But we must not expect finality. Bede was writing 300 years after the event. He knew nothing even of the history of his own province of Northumbria in the fifth century. If he records a popular tradition that the three English peoples once lived together he has told us something, and scraps of legend in Widsith, Beowulf, and the St. Alban's life of Offa give some colour for carrying their original homeland as far north as Bede's words will allow. Ethelweard and the Norman chroniclers, at least, took it that Jutland must be the land of the Iutae, though it must still be remembered that they are not independent witnesses. The evidence is that of Bede only, the choice of Jutland is an attractive amplification and no more, and Bede's words can be taken only as one of several echoes of folk tradition of remote antiquity.

Far more serious than our doubts of these wisps of tradition is the fact that by the middle of the fifth century most of the German races were so broken and diffused by migration that the question of ultimate origin has become of little importance. There were Saxons as far east as Merseburg, Angles between the Saale and the Unstrut, Angles, if Procopius, Adam of Bremen, and the *Lex Anglorum et Werinorum* can be trusted, in Torangia in the Rhenish delta. The impulse which took the English peoples to Britain was the last of a period of migration which had carried the Franks westwards and the Saxons and Angles far into the south, and the Jutes were no less restless and even more elusive.

There are several branches of the nation, though none of them in historical times were peoples of the north. In the fourth century a southern branch of Juthungi is found upon the Main and in association with the Alemanni. From the first century we have the Eudoses mentioned together with the Angli and Warni.[1] Both Procopius and the title of the somewhat later text of the *Lex Anglorum et Werinorum hoc est Turingorum* locate the Warni in Torangia in the Dutch Netherlands, touching the northern bank of the Rhine. Theudebert in his letter to Justinian claims the conquest of Pannonia, the land east of the lower Rhine in sixth-century language, *cum Saxonibus Euciis.* At about the period of the invasions, therefore, one tribe of Jutes seems to be placed at the centre of convergence of the Warni, Saxons, and Franks, roughly the Rhine valley from the inflow of the Ruhr to the Saxon lodgement upon the former river east of the Netherlands, and another to the south and east of the Franks upon the upper Rhine and the highlands lying to the east. Thus, were it not that the identification of Angulus with the Baltic peninsula is so universally accepted, one might be tempted to point out that a settlement of Angli and Warni at the Rhine mouth would be more truly *inter Iutarum et Saxonum provincias* than one in Schleswig, for it is of the Rhine settlement of the Saxons that Bede three times uses the phrase *antiqui Saxones* when writing of the actualities of his own day.

This is not a line which one would care to press seriously, partly because Bede's evidence as to the lie of the German peoples, *ex post facto* by 300 years, is not of great weight, and partly because from the very nature of our sources it must amount to special pleading. But it does raise a legitimate doubt as to whether Bede himself could have determined the precise moment of place and time in the wanderings of the three peoples at which the Angles lay between the Jutes and the Saxons, and whether we can erect his dictum into a prohibition of all search for the island Iutae elsewhere than in the Cimbric Chersonese. Perhaps this one identification has been given too much reality by its occurrence in our small canon of classical historians. We cannot read through the names of the Tribal Hidage without reflecting on the ephemeral life of some of our early racial names, or if we would see how others may persist long after they have lost their aptness, we may remember that in the thirteenth century the

[1] Tacitus, *Germania,* xl, c. 40.

ecclesiastical tenants of Cologne were still bound to voyage *ad Anglos vel Tenedos*, 'to the Angles and men of Thanet'. Some echo of the saga of Hengist and Vortigern, meaningless for 800 years, determined this conventional phrase of obligation. Bede, too, no doubt, had some such warrant for his tradition, some lay of Hengist or of Offa, but racial charts are not made from such evidence. These half-forgotten names and places are flimsy stuff to reason from.

It might be thought that language should make a clearer guide, but it does not. If the slightness of variation between the island dialects, hardly more than might be expected if so large a country had been covered by a single people in settlement, be considered, we might take it that Angle, Saxon, and Jute had a common home in Friesland. Yet Procopius is alone in including the Frisians among the invaders, so small a province is hardly likely to have poured forth so great a flood of emigrants, and if the one source of the English had been Friesland, Bede could hardly have failed to have said so, for he knew it well through the missions of Egbert to the Frisian king, Rathbod. Indeed, no explanation of the diffusion of dialects akin to that spoken in Frisia can be based upon any possible expansion of the Frisian nation as we know it in history, for it has been recorded, not only in all the English kingdoms, but in districts so remote as Dithmarsch and the Saale valley. We should do better with Mr. Chadwick's theory[1] of the primitive identity of the Frisian and Old Saxon tongues, for these at least were widely distributed in northern Germany. Even this, however, would leave the exceptional nature of Jutish institutions unexplained.

In reality, I think, the language question is not a crucial one. Even in the sixth century there are hints that the language of Kent was nearer to that of Franconia than of Wessex. Augustine could communicate with the Kentings through interpreters *de gente Francorum*, while a generation later Cenwall of Wessex dismissed his Frankish bishop *pertaesus barbarae loquelae*, and there are terms in the Kentish codes which are found in Frankish and not in Saxon sources. The Jutish settlement was small enough to take its

[1] H. M. Chadwick, *Origins of the English People.*

colour from the rest of England, and language is at best a fluid and transient test of nationality.

Nothing that can be advanced from contemporary literature or on the score of language can call for more than a suspended judgement upon the accepted theory, but it would not be worth while to disturb it were it not that archaeology has already found it necessary to dismiss a northern provenance for the Jutes and to look to a more southerly quarter, on the lower and middle Rhine.

The arts of Kent in the sixth and seventh centuries are of a type higher than, and very unlike those of their Saxon neighbours, and so, though with less distinction, are those of the western Jutish settlement of Hampshire. Whether by borrowing or from an amalgam of native impulses, Jutish artefacts have been found in considerable numbers in the burial sites of Sussex and Surrey. It is unnecessary to describe this art in detail: its wheel-turned pottery, its glass-ware, its characteristic use of garnet and crystal, are familiar to all. It is an art which, if it were unique, might be thought indigenous, the response of British provincial craft to the special taste and aptitudes of Jutish artists. Its type, however, is not confined to England. The grave-finds of the Ripuarian Franks stand in as marked a contrast to those of their neighbours, the Alemanni and Saxons, as do those of the island Saxons to the grave-finds of Kent, while the culture of the English Jutes and that of the Ripuarians are so closely similar as to make the identity of the two civilizations, if not of the two races, almost certain. 'It is in Frankish territory that the origin of most of the Kentish culture must be sought ... within a triangle at whose corners now stand the towns of Düsseldorf, Frankfurt, and Trier.'[1]

Mr. Leeds, to whom this identification is due, places the source of this stream of influence in the northern part of the Ripuarian power where Meckenheim, Nettersheim, Kärlich, Kruft, Niederbreisig, Niederdollendorf, and Andernach have yielded 'practically every single constituent that goes to make up the earliest culture of the Kentish cemeteries'. It is, therefore, a culture which is specifically Frankish, since it arises on the soil of their earliest settlement upon the Rhine.

[1] E. T. Leeds, *Archaeology of the Anglo-Saxon Invasions*, pp. 126, 128.

The identity of the British Iutae with the Franks seems not impossible on other grounds than that of art. Long established acceptance, minute as is the point from which it rises, makes it difficult to abandon the ingrained belief that all the Teutonic invaders came from the three small provinces about the Danish peninsula. Middle, almost southern, Germany seems an incongruous place in which to look for the provenance of an English race. And yet that incongruity is purely imaginary, an instance of the power of repetition to build up a fabric of pseudo-history which it is almost impossible to shake. If prejudice did not stand in the way, it would seem an impossibility that the vast movement of the Franks, which was flooding the Gallic province in the fifth century, which came in France and Belgium within a few hours' sail of Britain, should not have reached its nearest coast through the open gateway of the Rhine. To exclude the waves of conquest about the Channel, and to confine the English settlers to the most remotely northern of the many Anglian and Saxon provinces, is to go in the face of all contemporary likelihood.

Likelihood apart, no northern origin will account for the island Iutae upon the ground of fact. Search northern Germany as we will, we shall look in vain for any soil of custom upon which the civilization of Kent and its neighbours could have risen. It is all Saxon or Anglian ground, either in the *dorf* settlements of the country between the Weser and the Baltic or in the indefinite culture of several holding dominated by Saxon or Frisian admeasurement which lies between the Weser and the North Sea coast. The very foundation for a society which we could call Jutish first comes into sight where the Rhine turns southwards into the territory of the Franks. In all that district which Bede's tradition would allot to the Jutes and Angles, in all the great Saxon land from Schleswig to Thuringia, we have not the very elements from which to build up the system of our south-eastern provinces.

For many reasons, the full case for the Rhenish origin of the Kentings cannot be proved here. The detailed analysis which was necessary to show the nature of the lathe cannot be retailed again in a foreign setting, and the facts themselves are not all available. German scholarship has worked unremittingly upon field-forms and the details of agricultural practice, but it has made little of the relation of the cultivators to the state. A great deal of our proof must rest upon such evidence as German treatises can supply, and for the most part their untiring minuteness is devoted to a narrow field.

Yet the case is still a strong one. Negatively, it is, I think, conclusive. Kentish custom cannot have come from the north. When speaking of the contrast between the Jutish and Saxon agrarian plans it was unnecessary to enter into detail. The general build of the tenements was patently at variance. It may not, therefore, be realized how deep that contrast goes, how not only the build of the tenement and its place in the estate, but the place of every fraction in the tenement is determined by a complete and delicate articulation set once and for all by the custom under which the settlement was made, and startlingly different as between Jute and Saxon. The system by which the tenement is planned and admeasured reveals the antiquity and logical integrity of national custom.

Put simply, the contrast lies between the building up of the Saxon tenement from the strips of the open-field, and of that of the Jutes from units of ploughing capacity reckoned from the heavy team of eight oxen. In Wessex and in part of Mercia the basic unit is the yard or *virga*, the yard-width measured along the longer dimension of the quadrilateral of the open field. The tenement marked off by the customary number of such yards is the *yardland* or *virgata*, as being made up of the strips of which the yard forms the term. Thus the acre is a length of two yards along the field breadth but of uncertain depth and area.[1] The Kentish system, on the contrary, is not strictly a land measure, but one of labour. At its base is the unit of land covered by a day's ploughing, the *day-work* or *dieta*,[2] smaller than, but parallel to, the *jurnalis* or *morgen* of certain parts of the Continent, and it is built up

---

[1] This usage is well illustrated by a charter of Sutton by Crondal, Hampshire, where the boundary of 5 hides granted by Eadgar runs 'andlangas sledes syx aecera braede', the acre beng a lineal measure. *Cod. Dip.* DCXXIII.

[2] B.M. Add. MS. 37018, f. 67 b: 'Tenementum de Southerst jacet in Wynesberge et continet xxiv acras et j dietam'; P.R.O. Excheq. Augm. Off. M.B. 56, f. 123 b: 'In iij broklondes j acra j roda viij dayewerkes.' Excheq. T.R. 180, f. 136 (Lesnes).

into the normal tenement of the *jugum* or *yoke* of two oxen and the full *ploughland* or *sulung* of eight.

It is not to be denied that these terms are sometimes lightly used in the Middle Ages, that the time will come when a standard measure is necessary for the acre, and that upon the border-line of the two systems the terms virgate or hide may be loosely applied to what are in fact yokes and ploughlands, but the two scales of measurement are fundamentally opposed, and it must be evident that as the yardland is organically related to the open-field and its strips, so the yoke is inseparable from the assessment by the plough, and that neither unit can be divorced from the customary system of which it is a part. It is, for instance, a solecism to speak, as certain English historians have done, of the virgate as composed of 2 bovates—as well might one speak of the pound as divided into 12 inches—and too little weight has been given to these very searching criteria of custom. Their definition has been carried far farther in Germany than in England, notably by Professor K. Rhamm in his *Grosshufen der Nordgermanen*, and we can now see that they characterize the English races throughout their history and are as easily detectable in their pre-migration seats in Germany. This is particularly clear in that measurement by yards which we have seen to be proper to the strip system of the English Midland village, and for which German historians have found the name of *Breitensystem*. It is roughly Saxon in its distribution in Britain,[1] it is confined to north-west Germany on the Continent. Wherever it monopolizes the soil we cannot look for the homeland of the Kentings, or of any peoples less dominated by the sense of the soil than the Anglo-Saxons.

Now it may be said at once that the application of this test, and it is a test of the most pervasive and unchanging quality of the nation, puts out of court not only Jutland but the whole north of Germany as the place where the Jutes

[1] Our knowledge of the Anglian settlements in Britain is at present insufficient to enable us to define their agrarian scheme. Tradition would make the Northumbrians Angles rather than Saxons, but there they seem to have adopted the Celtic organization by ploughlands. Continental evidence suggests that they were in origin dorf-dwellers, not easily to be distinguished from the Saxons. There is an interesting field for inquiry here.

acquired that custom which they brought to England. Whether in the remote past they came from the north it is impossible to say, but Jutland as we know it is at the opposite pole of agrarian organization. Historically Jutland is, of course, Danish, but it is thought that the conquest may have begun as early as the third century, and though historians have detected pre-Danish survivals, they belong to the north-German type of the dorf. If, as is almost certain, the many sites qualified by the suffix -*syssel* perpetuate the 'settles' of the first inhabitants, their nucleated house-sites and open fields show them to be an extension of the villages of Saxon Germany. We are, in fact, in the heart of that great system of dorf settlement that covers the north of the later Saxon circle.

Equally unlikely is any other site from Schleswig to Thuringia. In the north-west of Germany we may find the closest of parallels with the field system of central England, but nothing which would justify us in linking that of our south-eastern counties with any surviving relics of the German past.

It would require many pages to reconstruct the systems of admeasurement which prevail in north Germany. The 800 pages of Rhamm and much of Maitzen's four volumes are devoted to it; a summary must suffice, and the verification of its fairness must be left to those who care to pursue the matter farther. The conclusions to be drawn seem to be these. The *Breitensystem*, the measurement by the width of the field-strip, with its units of the yard and yardland, virga and virgata, the outward sign of a regularly articulated system of open fields, is confined in its completeness in Britain to parts of Wessex and Mercia, with a doubtful incursion into Northumbria, and upon the Continent mainly to the north of the Weser, Holstein, Mecklenburg, Bremen, Friesland, and Oldenburg. In Dithmarsch the yard strip is built up into a peasant tenement, the *Jarde*, identical in name and function with the English *yardland*. In Friesland the peasant tenement is the *virga*, but the field system is too variable to be a sure guide. From all this we may extract the only two assurances that we need. First, that the Saxons of Wessex came from somewhere near the North Sea or Baltic coasts between the modern Holland and Pomerania, and secondly, that the *Iutarum natio* of Britain did not.

South and west of the Weser, stretching from Saxony to Hesse and reaching the line of the Harz mountains, we have a second tenemental system, but still one which bears no relation to that of Kent. Measurement is no longer by the strip, we are here in a country of enclosures, where open fields are rare, but the reckoning still deals with the soil. It is areal, not by real measurement, but by the estimated capacity of land, the so-called *Flächensystem*, good being brought into equality with bad by reckoning a smaller or larger area to the unit. The common base of the *morgen* is therefore spatially variable from village to village, and even from field to field. The whole system is ill-knit and irregular, has produced no uniform peasant tenement, and is only given a fictitious regularity by the imposition of a fiscal unit, the *hof*, for purposes of imperial taxes and dominical service. It reckons neither by the plough nor the field-strip, and stands in clear contrast to the more formally organized, though mutually incompatible, schemes of the English and German Saxons and of the Jutes. So indefinite a system invites caution in our judgement of it, but again we have nothing to suggest that we have come upon the homeland of our own south-eastern colonists. The north of Germany as a whole has yielded nothing.

A very different picture meets us in central western Germany. To begin with, we reach an ancient racial watershed at the line of the Rhine and Ruhr. The north at the end of the fourth century is mainly under the domination, racial and political, of the Saxons as leaders of the group of German peoples to whom Pliny and Tacitus give the name of Ingaevones. The same tradition allots the Rhineland to a separate racial stock, the Istaevones. Now, though the migrations have redistributed the balance within these two great groups and carried the Saxons and their allied peoples beyond their older boundaries at many points, the ancient frontier between the Ingaevones and Istaevones still survives, and corresponds with a marked cultural division during the Middle Ages, following roughly the course of the lower Rhine and the Ruhr, the northern boundary of the Frankish Empire. The Salian Franks occupy the northern half of the modern Belgium, the Ripuarians a narrow settlement of four provinces along the right bank of the middle Rhine from Frankfort to the Ardennes, and, to the west of the Rhine, the south-eastern Netherlands, the lower Mosel valley, and the subjected province of the Ubii in Jülich. The end of the fourth century is a moment of tension. The Saxons are at the end of their career of continental expansion, the Franks are about to begin the conquest of the West.

At this point upon the long journey across the face of Germany from the traditional home of the Iutae we enter for the first time a climate of custom in which we can feel our south-eastern colonists might once have lived. It is also the one area of Germany, the 'triangle at whose corners now stand the towns of Düsseldorf, Frankfurt, and Trier', whence the archaeologist can derive the distinctive arts of sixth-century Kent and southern Hampshire.

Beginning with Hesse and Frankish Thuringia south of the Harz mountains, we enter a country where the yard or acre as a strip of the open field or as a measured mass of land is unknown. Over the whole area of the middle Rhine, from the Mosel to the Main, the morgen or acre considered as the day's work of the plough is the rule, latinized as the *jugerum*, or in the vernacular as the *yoke, joch*, or *jeuch*. So in Kent also we have the *day-work* of the plough, the *dieta*, as the base of the table of land-measurement. Now, as the yard of the open field is built up into the peasant tenement of the yardland, the *virga* into the *virgata*, both in Wessex and in Old Saxony, so the natural multiple of the ploughing unit of the day-work or plough-acre should be the *ploughland*, both in Kent and the Rhineland. Universally in Kent, and sporadically in the Rhineland, where the purely fiscal and official unit of the *hoba*, the hof, does much to obscure it, we do in fact find the ploughland as the primary unit of admeasurement. In Kent the system is more perfectly articulated, for there, at least for the purposes of the Crown, the intermediate fraction of the jugum, the yoke or yokelet, breaks the sulung into quarters, while in the Rhineland, though the *juche*[1] appears as a substantial unit, it is not clear that it

[1] Beyer, *Mittelrheinisches Urkundenbuch*, ii. 354: 'Engelbertus dedit unum quod

occupies the same position as a fraction of the arable tenement as does the English *yoke*. Throughout the Ripuarian
provinces, however, beginning at the Netherlands border and
reaching as far south as Nassau on the east and Trier on the
west, the *terra aratri*[1] is widely spread, and is in itself, I
think, sufficient to prove the close relation of the tenemental
schemes of Kent and the Rhineland. The failure to build up
a substantial intermediate tenement like the Kentish yoke
is hardly a point of difference between the two systems, for
in Kent itself the subordination of the yoke to the sulung is
largely fictitious in historical times. Yoke and sulung seldom
exist together. Either the sulung, as in east and north, or
the jugum, as in west Kent, holds the field alone, and
beneath these primary units there is no subdivision short of
the acre or day-work. The tenements designated as juga or
terrae aratri in Kent might well exchange names, for there is
often very little difference in their size. That the *terra aratri*
should suffice to admeasure the Rhenish hamlets unsupported
by any fractional tenement is therefore no violation of the
system. In both countries partibility of inheritance has
brought about a great degree of amorcellation of the actual
holdings, particularly upon the smaller estates in lay hands,
the normal tenement tends to be irregular, and as long as the
ancient unit of the hoba or *terra aratri* holds together for
fiscal purposes internal subdivisions are of little importance
and can have little reality. The real identity of purpose and
working is vouched for by the identity of the two scales,
day-work, *acre*, *terra aratri* in Kent, *morgen*, *terra aratri* in
Ripuarian Germany.

Indeed, this is a land of enclosed settlement which, except
for the cultivation of the vine, takes its place in every way
with that of our south-eastern counties over against that of
the Saxon north. The hofs of the peasantry are like our

dicitur juch juxta Dudechinmulen et curtim pro filia' (Trier); ibid. ii. 420: 'In
Uffiningen . . . habet xiij juche de quibus predicto termino solvuntur v solidi et v
denarii' (Wittlich).

[1] Lamprecht, *Deutsches Wirtschaftsleben*, I. ii. 371: 'In Wulfesheim xvj mansos
de agricultura quantum ad aratrum sufficit' (Wörrstadt); 'Udewilre . . . ubi unius
aratri habeo agriculturam' (Lippe); ibid. I. ii. 704: 'Rethres . . . terra unius aratri
et prata et silva cum pascuis'; 'In Horowa vinea una et terra unius aratri'; 'In
Crufdelo terra unius aratri' (Hof Röders, Nassau).

Kentish hamlets—*hoba . . . cum casulis, pratis, sylvis*;[1] *hoba . . . cum mansis, casis, campis, vineis, silvis et foresta perfecta ad integro*;[2] they have their meadow, pasture, and wood in severalty and their share in the common forest. It is the ploughland as matrix of a fully equipped agricultural group, repeated upon German ground, as we have seen it in Kent.

Upon the soil of these two field systems, German and British, so alike in their potentialities, there rose a fabric of law to a large measure common to both peoples. By their very nature the written laws of the north have a certain likeness to each other. They record the essential for men who, of whatever race they might be, shared certain great principles of life. Whether with Norseman, Frank, or Saxon, the prime preoccupation of the age, peace and the just amendment of violent wrong, is the first and often the only matter of the code. The first effort of all written law is to make fixed and known the sums of gold, silver, or cattle by which the natural law of a life for a life may be appeased, 'the spear bought off', the feud laid. Difference shows as between nation and nation in the proportionate guilt which offences bear, and most of all in the value placed on the several ranks and orders of the folk. It is this scale of worth, in which the price of blood rises with the rank of him to whom wrong is done, which gives us our clearest view of primitive society. By it we can trace the affinities of the various political groupings and their relationship of race or culture.

We have something short of a dozen codes which may fairly claim to date from, or be representative of, the period of settled life which followed the migrations, and, spare as their record is, it is characteristic. The Saxon codes, whether of Old Saxony or Wessex, display the true notes of the Saxon polity as we know it from other sources, are in substantial agreement with each other, and have their differences from other laws in common. So it is with the rest, in so far as we have materials for judging.

The best touchstone of nationality in the simple lists of fines which are the basis of these codes is the *wergeld*. Against the extreme of violent death all ranks are protected with meticulous consideration of their standing, and so the

---

[1] Pardessus, *Diplomata*, dxciv.   [2] Ibid. lxxii.

estimate of nobility, simple freedom, or servitude is expressed with numerical precision. The principle is the same for every nation, but variety appears in the unit of calculation (the short hundred, or the long hundred of 120) and in the interval placed between the noble and the common free man.

In general, with certain variations of currency, the German peoples place a threefold fine upon the slaying of the noble or of the man in the following of the prince, and the reckoning is made by the long hundred of 120, but there are two striking exceptions or groups of exceptions. The Saxons, those of Old Saxony in the *Lex Saxonum*, and those of Wessex in the law of Ine, are unique in that they value the noble at six times the price of the free man, 1,200 shillings to 200 in the short hundred in Wessex, and 1,440 to 240 in the long hundred in Saxony. Both peoples, therefore, have the sixfold wergeld of the noble, though one reckons by the hundred of 120, the other by the decimal hundred, and since the lesser Wessex fines seem to be calculated to a duodecimal scale, we may believe that the two systems were at one time identical. The agreement of the blood-fines in the two branches of the Saxon people is, therefore, close enough to make us see in it the persistence of custom through the migration.

Equally striking is the identity of system between the Franks and the Kentings, a threefold wergeld for the noble going with a reckoning, unique in Germany, by the short hundred.[1] The Frankish *homo in truste regia* stands at 600 gold shillings to the ingenuus at 200,[2] the Kentish eorlcund-man at 300 gold shillings to the ceorl at 100.[3] This equivalence bears the stamp of historical origin in the use by both Franks and Kentings of a name for the blood-fine which is unique. In the last Kentish code the universal term of *wergeld* has already made its appearance; in that of Ethelbert it is still the Frankish *leude*, unknown otherwise in England

---

[1] Brunner in Pertz, *Leges*, ii. 52 n.   [2] *Lex Ripuaria*, xi.

[3] Seebohm, *Tribal custom in Anglo-Saxon Law*, p. 474, advances the view that the Kentish *leods* were of 600 and 200 shillings like the Frankish. It is difficult to disprove his case from the text of the Laws, but I think that the matter is finally disposed of by the mention of a wergeld of '2,000' in the will of the Kentish reeve Abba. This can only be a Kentish ceorl's wergeld of 100 shillings expressed in *sceattas*; cf. Chadwick, *Studies on Anglo-Saxon Institutions*, p. 22 n., and *Cart. Sax.* 412.

and peculiar in Germany to the Franks, that is used. He
who kills the king's freedman must pay the common blood-
fine, *meduma leodgelde*.[1] In this, as in the terms of Kentish
justice, the *sele*,[2] and the *medle*, and *thing*[3] as courts of law,
which have their Frankish, but not their English parallels
we may perhaps see the survivors of an older Frankish
terminology.

Upon the principal article of the wergeld, then, we have
two strongly identified unities, the Saxon group and the
most distinctly defined group of the Salians, Ripuarians, and
Kentings, and this is strong evidence of a common history.
The lesser offences and their amendments are less stable than
the *majores causae*, and are subject to adjustment in most
nations as the public conscience changes, but there are
points of identity between Franks and Kentings which seem
not to be accidental. The principal secondary wrongs, rape,
the loss of hand or eye, are the same, and stand at a half of the
wer instead of a third as in Wessex. The penalty for theft in
both is the full *wer*—one recalls the wergeld thief of the
charters—instead of the loss of hand or foot. The *wite* to
the Crown is half the value of the amendment to the kin in
homicide; in Wessex it is a quarter. Discrepancies occur,
but the whole impression conveyed by the British codes is
that the law of Ine is a variant upon the *Lex Saxonum*, the
laws of the Kentings varieties of a common type of which the
Frankish, and especially the Ripuarian code, are the other
nearest examples.

A conclusive proof of the common origin of Jute and
Frank calls for some such picture of the administrative
framework of the Rhine as we have been able to give of the
Kentish lathes. Unfortunately the full materials for such a
proof are not at present available, though what we have
points to some such scheme of provincial organization.

The initial problem would, of course, be to discover a
provincial unit capable of acting as an administrative, fiscal,
and judicial frame for such a polity—and the Rhineland has
at first sight no such distinctive unit as the rape or lathe. In
common with the rest of the Empire it lies under *pagi, gaue,*

---

[1] Ethelbert, 7; cf. also ibid. 23: 'þa magas healfne leod forgeldan.' *Lex Salica,*
xvi; *Capitulare* ii. 3. 8.   [2] Eadric and Hlothaere, 7.   [3] Ibid. 8.

and the gau is a province of indeterminate nature and widely differing extent. The Carolingian province may in fact perpetuate older provincial schemes or conceal them under new divisions, according to the particular district in question.

There is some reason for believing that the Rhineland may be one of those districts where the primitive scheme has suffered least disturbance. The *gau*, a name carried far and wide through Germany by the Carolingian conquests, seems to be native to the Franks, and, at least in the original homeland of the Ripuarians, it takes a form which in many ways recalls the lathe. As reorganized by Charles the Great, the Ripuarian gaue of the right bank of the Rhine, the seat of their first confederation, were four, Ruhrgau, Keldahgau, Deutzgau, Avelgau. Their size does not so far exceed those of the Kentish lathes as to make comparison impossible, and it may be that Charlemagne's constitution here and there joined smaller units to create the provinces between the Ruhr and the Main, as was done with certain gaue of the left bank. On the ground of extent, therefore, the Rhenish gau is better suited to act as the organizing unit of a folk than the use of the name in other parts of Germany might suggest, and there is in fact a possibility that the term itself was carried into Britain by the Jutes. Many years ago Professor Chadwick[1] observed the suggestion of identity between the suffixes of the earliest lathe names of Kent and the *-gau* termination of the Frankish pagi, and indeed the nomenclature of the river lathes taken as a whole is much like that of the Rhine. There we have Ruhrgau and Argau from the rivers Ruhr and Ara, in Kent we have Stur-geh[2] from the river Stour, which must have been the first name of the Borowara lathe before it took its name from the capital, and with it Limin-gae[3] from the Lymene, besides the less easily evaluated Eastorege.[4]

To determine how far this apparent identity in name between Kentish and Rhenish gaue stands for a real identity of institution would require a detailed study of the relation of the great prelatial estates, Köln, Mainz, Trier, Prüm, and so on, to the provincial administration, and this study has

[1] L. Chadwick, *Studies on Anglo-Saxon Institutions*, p. 253 n.
[2] *Cart. Sax.* 42.   [3] Ibid. 97, 98.   [4] Ibid. 318.

yet to be made. There is, however, much to suggest that
the Rhenish gau may have fulfilled a function like that of the
lathe. Service and custom, though more generally lapsed into
servitude than those of south-eastern Britain, preserve strong
elements of freedom and clearly derive from a Frankish
custom which was once generally free and akin to that of
Kent. The rules of inheritance, as recorded in the clauses
de alodibus of the *Lex Salica* and *Lex Ripuaria*, have the
same quality of freedom that we found in English peasant
right, and their rules for partition among heirs suggest that
the Franks of the sixth century were in process of transition
from a form of joint family holding to a partibility like that
of gavelkind. Arguing back from the *Constitutiones Cancie* of
the fourteenth century in the light of the strong status of the
kindred in Kentish custom, we might imagine an hypothetical section *de alodibus* for the code of Ethelbert which
would hardly differ from that of the *Lex Ripuaria*. With this
goes a common likeness in service. Peasant obligation in the
Rhineland, though heavier here and there than in south-
eastern Britain, is at times extraordinarily like that of the
greater Kentish manors. The custom of the prelatial lands
might often pass unnoticed in a custumal of Christchurch or
St. Augustine's, and might with no less reason be interpreted as the last phase of a provincial obligation under the
process of feudal disintegration.[1]

If the custom of the countryside was not unsuitable to
provincial organization it may also be said that the machinery
of the gau was not unsuited to exploit it. It has the same
judicial unity as we have found in the British provinces in
reeve, court, and capital township; in it the suffix *-heim* seems
to bear the same interpretation of an administrative centre to

---

[1] Beyer, *Mittelrheinisches Urkundenbuch*, i. 144: 'In banno Rethirrode habet
Archiepiscopus Trevirensis LXXV mansos quorum quilibet in festo S. Martini
solvit xiiij denarios Colonienses. In festo S. Andree quilibet solvit unum maldrum
avene Andernachensi mensure. Eodem termino vel postea quandocumque Archiepiscopus voluerit solvit ij gallinas. In Paschis xxx ora. Omnes mansionarii in isto
banno, exceptis scabinis et ministerialibus, tenentur una vice in anno domino
archiepiscopo cum plaustris unum iter facere vel ad Ohtinedinc vel monasterium
vel Cardon. Item quilibet mansionarius qui aratrum habet duobus diebus in anno
in hattis archiepiscopi arabit . . . Item eorundem mansionariorum quilibet dabit
archiepiscopo primo die ij messores . . . item quilibet triturabit una die.' (Rettherath
bei Virneburg, Kreis Mayen.)

a countryside of hamlets as that of -*hám* bears in Kent. Such centres as Oberenheim, *curia pupplica ducis, et sedes judicialis . . . ab antiquitate*,[1] might well change places with the Kentish *Roeginga hám* or the *regis oppidum Fefres hám*, if duke gave place to king. The judicial subdivisions of the gaue into *burgen*[2] like the English *borghi* and the late emergence of a unit of the *hundred* are at least remarkable as coincidences, even if more detailed examination should prove them to be accidental.

But among all these similarities the most striking is in the use of the woodland, and it is that which suggests most strongly that the gau once embodied the social life of a folk. It is clear from the *Lex Salica* and the *Lex Ripuaria* that the Franks used their forests in a manner identical with that of our south-eastern settlers. There is the same provincial reserve, the same common right of pasture passing at the edge of historical time into a pre-eminent right of the king and the growth of seignorial right under him,[3] and as each lathe or rape had its share in the Weald, so we are told the gau was the constituent unit through which was exploited the *silva communis* of the Franks.[4] It is this which imposes upon the Frankish deeds of the eighth century forms of conveyance which might pass in contemporary charters of Sussex, Kent, or Surrey. Recurrent grants of *mansi* with *silva ad eundem locum pertinens, cum terris eorum et portione silvae, cum silva ibidem aspiciente, cum foresta sua*, leave no doubt as to the identity of custom, and only the English technical terms of *dene* and *weald-bæru* are lacking to complete the parallel with an identity of form.[5]

Considered from every point of view, therefore, Frankish custom is compatible with an origin in the free status of the

---

[1] Pardessus, *Diplomata*, ii. 316.

[2] Lamprecht, *Deutsches Wirtschaftsleben*, I. i. 215.

[3] *Lex Ripuaria*, tit. 76: 'Si quis Ripuarius in silva commune seu regis . . . ligna abstulerit.'

[4] F. von Thudichum, *Geschichte des deutschen Privatrechts*, p. 76.

[5] Pardessus, *Diplomata*, cccxxxvi: 'Villa quae vocatur Templum Martis . . . cum pagena de silva de foresta nostra Windegonia'; ibid. ccclxii: 'Waerle . . . et silva ad eundem locum pertinens'; ibid. dxix: 'Rinharim . . . et portio mea in loco Haemoni, silva juris mei. In villa nostra Rinhari cassati quatuor cum terris . . . eorum et portiones de silva'; ibid. xxxvii: 'Haganbach . . . cum mansis, campis . . . aquis . . . cum foreste suo.'

folk, and the machinery is there to govern it upon that basis. The Rhenish gaue are large, but we may remember that the six Domesday lathes of Kent cover roughly double their number of older units, and the same kind of fusion may have been going on in the Rhineland at or before the time of the reorganization by Charlemagne. There seems no reason why we should not allot to the gau most of the functions of the lathe, and see in it the primitive marshalling of the Frankish folk.

Taken as a whole, the case for the derivation of the Jutish stock from the Frankish seems to me to be a strong one, and strongest upon the primitive ground of the Ripuarian settlement. There the *Lex Ripuaria* stands nearest to the Kentish codes, the custom of the ecclesiastical estates is most akin to that of gavelkind, the exploitation of the forest is most like that of south-eastern Britain, the form of the gau is nearest that of the lathe, and above all the art of the grave-finds is most closely akin to that of our southern coasts. At this point, the triangle between Düsseldorf, Mainz, and Trier, law, agrarian practice, and custom unite in a common verdict in agreement with that of archaeology, and the concurrence of so many lines of evidence constitutes a strong claim to acceptance.

It is evident that the Rhine valley at the turn of the fourth and fifth centuries offers a fair opportunity for a compromise judgement. This is the pivot of time and place upon which the great movements of the northern peoples turn, and the junction to which the two great racial stocks of Ingaevones and Istaevones converge. With the former we must associate the Saxons of Britain by their threefold identity in language, art, and custom, with the latter we must associate the British Jutes by their art, and by their custom, but not by their language, which we have only slight reasons for detaching from the common stock of the Island Saxons. The Saxons have reached the Rhine in the eastern Netherlands. There are Warni, and because the Angli and Warni are closely associated, we must believe Angli also, about the Rhine mouth, and the Franks were at war with them here in the last decade of the fourth century. The southern Eucii appear in the first half of the sixth century as a buffer state between Franks and Saxons. Finally, the Salian Franks from Brabant are on the point of beginning their conquest of Gaul at the expense of both Saxons and provincials, and the Ripuarians have just completed an expansion which has brought them to the borders of both Saxon and Salians upon the middle Rhine. In short the whole lower and middle Rhine basin is the scene of contact and rivalry between the Ingaevonian and Istaevonian races, the former at the end, the latter at the beginning of their greatest periods of conquest.

There is much material here for a theory which would smother all difficulties by assuming an amalgam of invaders, in swift conquest or piecemeal settlement, across the narrow seas, a movement which should emerge from the open gateway of the Rhine delta, after drawing upon the cultural and racial stocks which meet upon its banks, Saxon north and Frankish south. Frankish custom and Saxon-Friesian language would not be impossible as the result of such confusion, and even the name of Eucii might be salved from this convenient stream of flotsam.

On the whole, however, such a solution raises more difficulties than it solves. Some, who think that a century of neighbourhood in Britain will not explain the fact that the Jutes speak the common language of England, may be ready to believe that the peasantry of the south-east were Frisians, Saxons, Angles, Warni, with Frankish leaders and Frankish art and organization, perhaps with the elusive Saxones Eucii among them, but the fact has to be faced that there is nothing but language to suggest it. The art of the south-east seems to be purely Frankish and so does its custom as we see it in its purity in the Kentish codes and custumals, and the grafting of custom so complex and many-threaded seems impossible. The settlers of the Saxon enclave in Sussex may well have been swept into a Frankish enterprise from their recorded settlements on the coast of Picardy, but here, as we might expect, there was little interchange of custom. Either race kept its social build unaltered, so far as life under a common administration would permit. Jutish custom in Britain seems to be intact from king to peasant, and the one close parallel to it is the Frankish. Compromise, then, seems to be difficult, and short of some revolutionary discovery within the sphere of the Frisians or Warni, a discovery which the thoroughness of the work already done by Hest makes unlikely, it is to the middle rather than to the lower Rhine that we must look for the eventual impetus towards the first settlement of Britain. Whatever our judgement on this may be, the north is beyond consideration. Our settlers came from within the Frankish influence, if not from within the Frankish homeland.

There the problem must for the moment rest—upon probability and conjecture. The picture seems to me a more acceptable one than that to which we are accustomed, the change of viewpoint to be one that is worth the making. The district of the south-east is a crucial one for our knowledge of the invasions. The whole of English history gains in meaning by every step towards the discovery of the origins of the English people. If the analysis which I have attempted be a true one, even in its general outline, the earliest phase of the Teutonic conquest becomes intelligible to a degree to which it has not been so before. The legend of small and unconnected adventures, Saxon or otherwise, cruising in vacancy till they come to a lodgement in Kent or Sussex, or in Hampshire, has never seemed convincing. The scale should be larger to fit a stage upon which whole peoples were in migration. The wanderings of the races as we know them upon the Continent require as their English parallel some widespread movement in which both shores of the Channel are involved in a common settlement, and in assigning a larger sphere to the civilization of Kent we are bringing a great part of the English peoples into an understandable relation to the nearest of their continental neighbours. The attack upon Britain, if rightly timed about the traditional date of A.D. 449, chimes too well with the first great conquests of the Franks to be without relation to them. The spring of race and culture for all this part of England might well to all appearances have risen in the Rhine, and the Frankish advance to the westward, which flooded northern France and the Netherlands and founded the Toxandrian kingdom in the fourth century, would not easily be stayed from crossing the narrow seaway in the fifth. It is in some such extension of the general catastrophe, and not in the casual raids of northern rovers, that we should expect the end of the British province to come.

But the real gain is not here. Who the Jutes were is not of vast importance, and English history would be much the same whether they came from north or south. But to establish a free constitution in the fifth and sixth centuries is of very great importance indeed, and if it were accepted much of our later institutional history would change its colour. Indeed, any clear view of the beginnings of England should be of value. It is vital to find some intelligible organization of life behind the apparently solid barrier of Saxon feudalism. Unlike that of all other western nations, our history has always begun upon a question. England did not rise out of the even flow of the Latin tradition. The Roman continuity was broken. But equally the debased and highly artificial structure of Saxon manorialism has seemed to bar the channels to the genius of the northern world. The instinct which led Freeman to exaggerate every trait of Teutonic sentiment was an historically sound one, though the proof of its rightness was not then to hand. A nation of lords and serfs could never have carried into the Middle Ages that deep sense of individual worth and communal integrity which led through the legal popularism of Henry II to a Parliament which was the grand inquest of the nation. In the fifth century these were barbarian and, for that reason, Teutonic virtues, and no history of the foundations of England will be credible which does not show a state and a society such as could have been vehicles and fit transmitters of this northern tradition. If we can pierce behind economic and social feudalism to a commonwealth which still lives in, and is governed by, the franchise of its common folk, we shall have swung English history back into its true line of inheritance, and the way will be open for a fuller sense of the legal and political vitality of the English countryside. Provincial government as I have described it will do this for at least one quarter of England. The lathe and the rape show how life in that primitive age could be lived without servitude, without debasing inequality, and yet preserve a fabric of order, adequately protected justice, and continuity. In thinking of the age of settlement we need not really choose between economic feudalism and a vaguely defined notion of tribal anarchy. Rather, we should think of a simply organized but stable state, a federation of folks in their provinces, for the most part under kingship, though here and there history shows that kingship was not essential, in which most men were free and every free man was folk-worthy, mot-worthy, and fyrd-worthy. In this society, a natural outcome of the age before the migration as after it, we may see the open course by which Teutonic custom flowed into English custom, and the memory and use of law and the potentiality of political action were transmitted from their common source in the north. The Jutish provincial scheme is typical of an unrealized phase of our history and of that in which the promise of our political genius was in the making.

It is to this general task of illuminating the pre-feudal phase in English history that my mind has been turned in preparing these pages, and not to the specific problem of the Jutes alone. They are, indeed, interesting chiefly as one instance of an era of history, the age of settled life that intervened between the migratory phase of the tribe and the coming of feudalism. The balance of freedom and stability reached by our south-eastern settlers could be, and, I have no doubt, was achieved upon somewhat similar lines elsewhere, but this is our type. Jutish civilization, in so far as it has a unity, is significant as an example of how life could be organized in the pre-feudal age—the age before the famous transition from status to contract.

THE HUNDRED IN KENT

In this study of Kentish institutions the hundred is only mentioned in passing. I believe it to be an alien intruder of the tenth century, but to prove it to be so would have broken the thread of continuity with a long and purely negative exposition. I preferred therefore to reserve the subject for a separate study, and to confine the matter here to the limits of a short appendix.

Briefly, the case against a native origin for the Kentish hundred is as follows. Its existence before the West Saxon conquest is almost verbally denied by charter evidence. Until the tenth century land is always described by its position as dependent upon one of the lathe capitals or within one of the lathes, although it may not be in the medieval hundred in which the capital lies. Graveney is in Boughton Hundred in Domesday, but in 812 it is 'in partibus suburbanis regio oppidulo Fefresham', and a roughly contemporary charter shows the 'regio on Liminum' extending over the site of the later hundred of Hen. Again, unlike the lathe, unlike so many hundreds in Wessex and Mercia, the Kentish hundreds possess neither uniformity nor permanence. They range in area from the 61¾ sulungs of Hoo to the single jugum of Wachelestan. Quite plainly they did not present themselves as units to the men who planned the hidation, and during the Middle Ages they change their boundaries, divide and combine in a way which proves them to have no deep hold as institutions.

In fact their function was closely restricted. Except for such hundreds as embody one of the ancient royal seats of justice and so hold its pleas, they have no jurisdiction save the comparatively late developed process of infangthef; they meet only for the view of frankpledge and 'pro latrone judicando', and I am led by these facts to consider the Kentish hundred as essentially a court for the almost universal baronial franchise of infangthef, and an administrative unit for the equally widespread immunity of frankpledge, and this is confirmed by the extraordinarily close identity of the hundreds with the greater manors or honours. The outlines of the Kentish hundreds owe their variety and completely disparate proportions to the natural inequalities of the map of lordship. The hundred seems to have grown up with manorial feudalism, and to be confined to the pleas enjoyed by the feudatories. Especially is it identified with the jurisdiction and administration of thief-taking, and I am inclined to associate it with the hundredal regulation of the punishment of theft which was carried through in the reigns of Edmund and his immediate successors. A

West Saxon origin at that period would solve almost all the outstanding problems of its form and function, and the map of hundredal lordship is to all appearances one which could only have come into being by the imposition of hundredal franchise upon a grouping of estates which we can see coming into being in the charters of the ninth and tenth centuries.

This is a subject to which I hope shortly to recur elsewhere, and I offer this abstract only in justification of my belief that the hundred has no place in the story of Kentish institutions, and of its consequent omission from this study.